short cuts to
BEAUTIFUL
GARDENS

short cuts to
BEAUTIFUL GARDENS

DAVID SQUIRE

CASSELL
ILLUSTRATED

First published in paperback in 2003 by Cassell Illustrated
A Member of the Octopus Publishing Group Ltd
2-4 Heron Quays
London
E14 4JP

Distributed in the United States of America by
Sterling Publishing Co., Inc.,
387 Park Avenue South, New York, NY 10016-8810

A CIP catalogue record for this book is available from the British Library.

1 84403 034 2

Printed in Slovenia

Publisher's note
Throughout this book, the very best of the many short cuts and tips
featured are either presented in tinted boxes or denoted by a grey or
black bullet in the text.

Frontispiece: A richly planted spring border is the epitome of what makes a
beautiful garden. It need not take much time and effort to create such an
effect.

Contents

Introduction

Gardening is an intensely creative and personal pursuit, all about experimentation, the adoption of new ideas and above all working with Nature – yet at the same time trying to harness and surpass her best endeavours. It is also a constant battle against some of Nature's worst excesses, namely the vagaries of weather, such as too much sun, excessive rain and low temperatures.

Few gardens offer that much eulogized 'deep, friable loam' in which roots love to roam and seeds are eager to germinate. Instead, there is often the jaundiced inheritance of a soil that bakes hard in summer, oozes with water in winter, or is so light and sandy that moisture-retention is limited and nothing will grow. Yet throughout each year keen gardeners tirelessly tend their gardens and look for inspirational ways to improve them....

So is gardening a labour of love, with the accent firmly on labour? It need not be. Although very often good gardening involves a lot of blood, sweat and tears – while at the same time hurting the pocket – it is possible to modify and improve existing gardens beyond recognition in a variety of quick and easy ways. This book is packed with ideas, tips and short cuts that will enhance any garden, without taking too much of the owner's time and energy in the process. It will show you how to assess what is best in your garden and what you should keep, while revealing simple solutions to the common problems that afflict nearly every garden.

There are innovative planting schemes that will work just about anywhere, ideas for easily-built decorative features that will transform a garden's entire structure, quick-fix ideas and tips that will help you renew and improve the many different elements that make up a good garden. Discover how to create rapid year-round colour with the minimum of effort, how to personalize your garden with distinctive ornaments and embellishments and, most of all, how to make the most of the precious hours you spend in the place that most defines the entire context of your home. Your garden can be beautiful, and it need not take forever. Read on....

Opposite: Everybody wants a beautiful garden – the right balance of plants and other features to create aesthetic harmony and a unity of design. It need not always be hard work to achieve this goal – there are lots of short cuts.

New names for old

Throughout this book the most recent botanical names have been used for plants, but where an earlier name is better-known and still used, this too is mentioned.

Gardeners are often conservative by nature and tend to use botanical names learned years ago. Consequently, it can be confusing when plant names are changed. By listing both recent and earlier names, this book aims to avoid confusion and can also help in the identification of plants mentioned in other old but still valued gardening books.

Even current seed and plant catalogues do not always list up-to-date botanical names: sensibly, seedsmen and nurserymen are more eager to make plants known to prospective customers than they are in compiling a list of correct botanical names. However, there must be a balance between these two approaches, and for that reason this book gives both current and previously-used botanical names.

Garden therapy

Beautiful summer flowers enhance the borders of any garden. Here, the summer annuals *calendula*, *cosmos, tagetes* and *zinnia* have been interplanted to great effect.

Gardening is both an evolutionary and innovative process. It is possible, of course, to buy a house where the garden is established and already bursting with colour. But after a few months it is inevitable that thoughts of tailoring the garden to your own and your family's needs will come to the fore. Ideas may include adding windowboxes, hanging-baskets and plants in tubs and pots to a patio, perhaps creating a cartwheel herb garden, or planting colourful summer-flowering borders.

Improving existing features

There are numerous different ways of improving a garden, but adding further plants that will grow flowers or attractive foliage throughout the year and renovating features that are already present are the most obvious starting-points. Decorating

neglected patios and lawns will soon brighten a garden and create attractive foils for border plants, shrubs and trees.

Most gardens have lawn edges that need tidying up; for rapid enhancement of the whole garden, broken ones can be repaired and ornamental edgings installed (see page 119). Also, those edges alongside walls or borders can be made easier to cut by installing a mowing strip, formed of either paving slabs or a gulley filled with shingle.

When taking over a new garden it is possible that shrubs and hedges have been neglected. Often, the first reaction is to dig them up, but it may be possible to give them a fresh appearance and a new lease of life through radical pruning. Detailed advice on how to renovate shrubs and hedges is given in Chapter 3.

Mixing and matching plants

Creating groups of plants that produce colourful displays is essential to the establishment of a successful small garden. Attractive planting combinations can be achieved with many different types of plants, including bulbs, herbaceous perennials, annuals, biennials, shrubs and trees. Throughout this book, combinations of plants are suggested, from small corners sown with hardy annuals to herbaceous borders and medleys of bulbs under trees. There are even suggestions for combinations of plants that will provide colour and bring cheer during winter.

Planting climbers in exciting combinations is a part of this book, as well as how to mix roses effectively with other plants. All of these innovations can be achieved quickly and easily and all of them help to create a bright and genuinely personalized garden.

Colour harmonies and contrasts are important in the garden, especially on patios and around houses where plants can be selected to create superb displays in the form of backgrounds to these man-made features. Colourful spring and summer

combinations are suggested for a whole range of different climbers, suitable for decorating white-washed walls, grey stone walls or those built of red brick.

Seasonal and scented gardens

Gardens are usually at their best during summer, but it is possible to buy and cultivate plants that will enliven gardens from autumn to spring, some of which also offer exciting fragrances. Many trees and shrubs yield colourful fruits and some persist from autumn to late winter, while a wide range of shrubs reveal flowers during winter. Spring, of course, is a time for bulbs, and perhaps daffodils are the best known harbingers of the season. Several miniature bulbs brighten winter, such as the well-known and ever-popular snowdrop, while the goblet-shaped flowers of *Crocus chrysanthus* form a dazzling display when planted in large groups naturalized in lawns, or under deciduous trees, such as silver birch.

Ideas for plants to choose in order to create colourful displays of flowers and foliage in containers on patios are abundant throughout the following chapters, as well as those that can be used to brighten porches and other entrances. In

Cortaderia selloana – **pampas grass – provides a majestic and hardy foil to many different plants. It looks especially effective in full autumn bloom alongside dramatically coloured foliage.**

An attractive oriental-style sunhouse creates an unusual and interesting feature. Surround it with a variety of containers, and it will immediately make a huge visual impact on the entire garden.

Opposite: It takes a little time to create a garden as harmonious and well-established as this one, but with careful planning and the application of some well-chosen tips, even the busiest hobby gardener can aspire to such effects without *too* much effort.

addition, there are many plants that can be quickly and easily planted in windowboxes to produce rich fragrances and effects that are vastly disproportionate to the effort and expense involved; some of these are seasonal but by using separate displays for winter, spring and summer, scents can be produced throughout the year.

Fragrance is a wonderful medium for enhancing any garden. Roses are often chosen for their perfumes, and apart from a rich sweetness, many reveal unusual scents, such as apple, musk, myrrh, orange, paeony, primrose and sweet pea. A few climbers are known for their delicate scents, while wisterias produce a penetrating vanilla-like fragrance; many of these plants are featured in this book.

Awkward corners

Few gardens are free of awkward areas – those that suffer from direct and scorching sunlight, total shade, wind or coastal salt-spray. Plants that thrive in these places and will quickly create attractive displays are featured in this book, and some of them will even help to prevent the growth of weeds.

Hedges for all gardens – whether to produce screens of attractive foliage or flowers, or to reduce wind interference and generally create a more congenial ambience – are also suggested. Their growing times, heights, spreads and pruning requirements are all discussed in detail, with the objective of keeping time and effort to a minimum always in mind.

Quick ways to brighten gardens

There are many especially quick and inexpensive ways to improve gardens, and a range of these are featured in this book. Tired old lawns and patios, bumpy drives and paths, tatty old garden furniture in need of refurbishment – all these things detract massively from the overall visual effect of a garden, but all of them can be improved and enhanced in no time at all. This book will show you how.

Making a Start

When you are setting out to improve your garden, the first thing to do is to make an overall assessment of both its good and bad features. There are many things to consider – from the nature of the soil and the quality of existing plants to the state of prominent features such as sheds and greenhouses. Fortunately, there are many ways in which a garden's faults can be rectified and turned to your advantage – and often very quickly.

It is the main visual perspective in a garden that is responsible for its overall effect. In the past many gardens were planned around the most mundane of items – a straight washing-line. A long path accompanied the line, and thus the entire perspective of the garden was dictated. With the introduction of rotary washing 'spinners', however, the form of gardens became less formal. Changing the orientation of a summer-house or greenhouse can have much the same effect.

What are the dominant features of your garden, and what state are they in? Here, these overgrown steps and scruffy old plantings need some work.

Assessing your garden

Getting to know your garden's basics – its soil, topography and general orientation – will help you identify its poor qualities and learn more quickly how to take advantage of its good ones.

Living with your soil

The top 30cm (12in) of soil can usually be improved annually and made suitable for a wide range of plants – especially vegetables and summer- and spring-flowering bedding plants. However, for plants with a longer lifespan, such as herbaceous perennials and shrubs, trees and hedges, it is easier to cultivate new hardy plants that will tolerate extremes of conditions (see Chapter 3).

A garden's size and shape

Your perception of your garden's size and shape changes throughout the year, as the seasons turn. However, if the garden is old and neglected or has an inherently dull and claustrophobic nature, it will never naturally improve itself that much. Yet remove just a few shrubs or trees – having chosen judiciously – and the entire garden will regain space and vibrancy. Even simply removing a few branches from a large tree can make a radical difference.

   Tall, dominant hedges create a closed, oppressive ambience and are best removed. As an alternative to a hedge, consider a free-standing trellis, 1.5–1.8m (5–6ft) high and clad in foliage or flowering climbers. In areas buffeted by strong winter winds, choose deciduous climbers that do not create a 'solid', closeting screen throughout the year. Position such a trellis about 45cm (1½ft) from the boundary, so that it can be maintained and plants from the trellis do not invade your neighbour's garden.

Strong colour and form in trees and shrubs are blessings in any garden. Think twice before removing such key visual elements.

Digging up a tree or hedge

If you do decide to cut down a tree or hedge, do not immediately sever it at ground level. Instead, cut the trunk 1.8–2.1m (6–7ft) above the ground, but not so high as to make the cutting operation uncomfortable for you. Dig a trench around the tree and use the long trunk as a lever to loosen the roots. They can then be cut with an axe or saw.

Old plants in a new garden

Whenever moving house presents a gardener with an existing garden packed with shrubs, trees and climbers, the questions 'are they too old and overgrown?' and 'should they be dug up?' immediately spring to mind. If the plant is in the right position, but overgrown, do not remove it but rather prune it . You may have second thoughts about the plant after a while, but initially do not remove plants that can be rejuvenated.

Rejuvenating neglected shrubs

Many old, neglected shrubs are large and unsightly, swamped with foliage and covered with shoots that produce few flowers. Neglected hedges can also become excessively large, excluding light and robbing the soil of moisture and food. Here are a few ways to quickly give common shrubs a new lease of life:

***Aucuba japonica* 'Variegata' (spotted laurel):** Cut back overgrown shrubs to about 60cm (2ft) above the ground in spring.

Berberis: Usually, no regular pruning is needed but, where growth is congested, cut back old or exhausted shoots to ground level or healthy main shoots. Prune evergreen species as soon as their flowers fade; prune deciduous types in late winter.

***Buddleja davidii* (butterfly bush):** Where yearly pruning has been neglected, in spring use secateurs or a saw to cut back all of the previous season's shoots to within 5–7.5cm (2–3in) of the older wood.

***Choisya ternata* (Mexican orange blossom):** Cut back excessively large and neglected bushes with secateurs in late spring. This usually means losing the subsequent summer's flowers.

***Cornus* (dogwood):** Where shrubs are used to create coloured shoots – and have been neglected – use strong secateurs or a saw to cut all stems to within 5cm (2in) of the ground in early spring.

***Forsythia* (golden bells):** Where shrubs have been neglected, use secateurs or a saw to cut out old wood in spring.

***Hypericum calycinum* (rose of Sharon):** Where plants have become rampant, cut all shoots to within 7.5cm (3in) of the ground in early or mid-spring.

***Kerria japonica* (Jew's mallow):** Where plants create a forest of neglected shoots, cut them all just above soil-level after their flowers fade.

***Laurus nobilis* (bay laurel):** Use sharp secateurs or a saw to cut back neglected and old shrubs in spring.

Living with old climbers

Old, rampaging climbers are often a danger to the fabric of a house. The shoots and leaves of ivies block guttering and down pipes, while wisteria shoots delve behind old and loose beams on the outsides of houses. Ivies that clamber up colour-washed, pebble-dashed walls make re-painting difficult and can also undermine plaster and loosen the surface to be painted. Climbers like these are best removed or radically pruned before they create further damage.

Lavandula **(lavender):** Use secateurs to cut back straggly plants in spring to encourage the growth of fresh shoots.

Potentilla **(shrubby cinquefoil):** Neglected plants produce long, straggly stems. Cut these back to their bases when the flowers fade.

Rhododendron: Where plants are exceptionally large and leggy, cut them back in mid-spring – if necessary, to about 30cm (12in) above the soil.

Syringa **(lilac):** Where shrubs are old and neglected, rejuvenate them by cutting the entire plant to 60–90cm (2–3ft) above the ground in mid-spring.

Rejuvenating neglected hedges

Crataegus monogyna **(hawthorn):** Cut back all branches in late summer; fresh shoots will develop during the following spring.

Ilex **(holly):** Use secateurs to cut back excessively large holly hedges in spring.

Lavandula **(lavender):** Use secateurs to cut back straggly plants in spring to encourage the growth of fresh shoots.

Ligustrum **(privet):** Use secateurs or a saw to cut back excessively large hedges in spring. It may take a full season for the hedge to create fresh growth.

Prunus laurocerasus **(common laurel):** Use secateurs – and even a saw – to cut back excessively large hedges in spring.

Rosmarinus officinalis **(rosemary):** Where plants are overgrown, use secateurs to cut back all shoots by half in mid-spring.

Moving daffodils and tulips

If you move to a new garden in spring or early summer, it is likely that you will inherit daffodils or tulips in flower. If you wish to move them to another area, dig them up after their flowers fade and bury their bulbs and lower stems in a trench dug in an out-of-the-way corner. Allow the foliage to die down, then remove the bulbs, store in boxes and replant in late summer or early autumn. (See illustrations page 21.)

Well-established plants give a garden character, even if they have seen better days. It is quicker and easier to rejuvenate them than to re-plant.

This floriferous clematis in a container could be used as an attractive replacement for old wall climbers that are beyond help.

Personalizing your garden

There are countless different ways to personalize your garden and make it stand out, from adding a few plants in attractive pots on a patio to creating a chamomile lawn.

Creating edgings: The edges of paths need not be dull. In Victorian times ornate tiles were popular – and they are still available. Plain, rounded, rope-finished and other ornate designs are still sold; they can be quickly installed alongside a path.

Log steps: These are ideal for informal, woodland settings; they are quickly and easily constructed, without the need for mixing concrete. The logs are held in place with long, stout pegs which are hammered into the soil.

Retaining walls: Informal retaining walls planted with rock garden plants always create colourful features, especially in spring. Ensure that the wall leans slightly backwards and that there is plenty of drainage material behind the wall. Also, there must be drainage holes left at the base of the wall.

Rose tripods: If a trellis, wall or fence is not available, grow roses up tripods. These are formed of three 2.4m (8ft) long planed pieces of wood erected like a wigwam and about 1.2m (4ft) wide at their base. Alternatively, use a thick, single pole secured in a hole. If the pole has short sideshoots left on it, these provide further

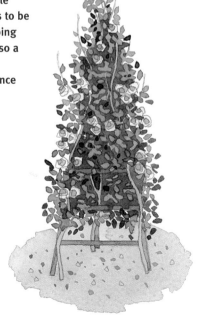

Rose tripods enable interesting shapes to be created with climbing roses. They are also a good medium for introducing fragrance into the garden.

Retaining walls make a huge impact in the garden when sumptuously planted up with trailing rock garden plants.

support for the rose's stems. Varieties of roses to choose include:

'Aloha': Clear salmon-pink and rose
'Copenhagen': Dark scarlet
'Dreaming Spires': Yellow
'Golden Showers': Golden yellow
'New Dawn': Silvery-pink
'White Cockade': Pure white

Sundials and armillary spheres: As a centrepiece in a large lawn, a sundial or armillary sphere has few rivals. It needs to be displayed on a round dais of ornate bricks or crazy-paving.

Chamomile lawns: These must be considered as decorative features, and not hard-wearing surfaces for family use. Use the non-flowering form of the plant *Chamaemelum nobile* 'Treneague' – when crushed, its foliage has the fragrance of bananas and apples. Space plants 10–15cm (4–6in) apart in spring. When 7.5cm (3in) high, cut off their tips.

Thyme paths: Like chamomile, thyme can be used to create an aromatic lawn; it can also be employed to form a fragrant path.

To create a thyme path, dig an area 90cm–1.2m (3–4ft) wide and the path's length. Systematically tread over the surface to firm the soil evenly; install stepping-stones along it. Then, plant thyme 20–25cm (8–10in) apart.

Unusual paths: When reconstructing an old path, consider medleys of different materials laid in interesting patterns, to bring greater variety to the garden.

Weeping standard roses: These create spectacular features in rose borders or as centrepieces in lawns. They are formed when two or three buds of a suitable variety are budded on to a stem of a rootstock 51cm (1¾ft) above the ground. This produces a flowering head, packed with flowers, 1.5–1.8m (5–6ft) high. Suitable varieties include:

'Albéric Barbier': Cream
'Crimson Showers': Crimson
'Goldfinch': Yellow
'Sander's White': White

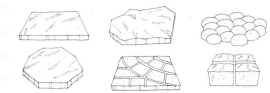

One of the most noticeable features of any garden is the type of paving used in paths or patios. Give your garden a touch of individuality with different stones.

Like path or patio surfaces, path edgings can make all the difference without being especially difficult to install. Many different shapes are widely available.

If you want a dramatic centrepiece to transform your garden, look no further than a sundial.

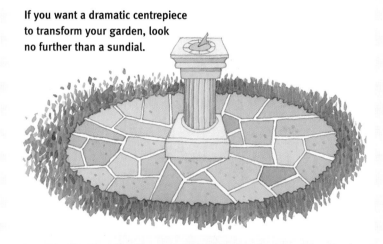

Wildflower gardens: Apart from creating colourful areas, wildflower gardens attract native birds and insects. Suitable seed mixtures can be bought cheaply.

Wildlife ponds: These are quite different from traditional garden ponds, which usually involve simple stocks of plants and fish. Wildlife ponds are meant to be havens for native birds, fish, small mammals, amphibians and insects. This type of pond is easily made from a flexible liner spread over a hole. Create a bog garden at one end, and moisture-loving marginal plants can also be grown. (See illustration page 76.)

Quick ways to improve gardens

If your garden is neat and tidy, it will generally create a good first impression. On the other hand, signs of neglect – such as an unkempt lawn with broken edges – immediately spoil the effect. Here are a few quick fixes...

Lawns – broken edges: Where an edge has been damaged, place a piece of wood 20–23cm (8–9in) wide, 30cm (12in) long and 6–12mm (¼–½in) thick over the damaged area and with the short side flush with the lawn's edge. Use an edging-iron (also known as an edging-knife) to cut around the board. Then, cut evenly under it with a spade. Lift out the complete turf and reverse it, so that the damaged area faces inwards. Firm the turf and fill and firm the broken part with compost; sprinkle with grass seed, rake level and gently water.

Lawns – holes in the turf: These immediately detract from a lawn's appearance, but can be quickly levelled. Place a piece of wood about 23cm (9in) square and 6–12mm (¼–½in) thick over the hole and use an edging-iron to cut around it. Use a spade to remove the piece of turf. Then, use the same piece of wood to cut a fresh, undamaged piece of turf from an out-of-the-way position; place it in the hole and check that it is level. Firm it and trickle compost into the cracks. Thoroughly water the entire area.

Lawns – hollows and bumps: If not more than 1.2m (4ft) across, these can be easily levelled. Stretch a garden line over the centre of the depression or mound and use an edging-iron to cut the turf to about 5cm (2in) deep (see diagram, left). Then, measure 30cm (12in) wide strips at right-angles to the base line and cut along them. Cut under the turves with a spade and roll them back. Remove or add compost to level the surface, then roll back the turves. Firm them, trickle compost between the joints and water the entire area.

Fences – broken posts: Where posts have rotted at ground level, dig out the decayed part and position a concrete spur so that it

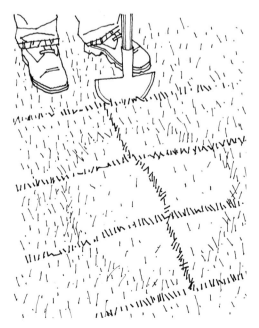

Correcting hollows and bumps in lawns does not take long and will make a significant difference to the overall look of the garden.

rests against the top part of the post. Check it is upright, drill the wooden post and bolt it to the concrete spur. Secure the post upright, ram hardcore around the spur's base and then add concrete. (See diagram, right.)

Fences – broken arris rail: Where one of these rails rots at the position it joins a supporting post, install a proprietary galvanized bracket. Use galvanized screws to secure it. (See diagram, far right.)

Paths – broken and badly positioned: Any path's surface will eventually deteriorate with age and its foundations will crumble. When this happens, it presents a golden opportunity to remove the path entirely and to create an entirely different garden, perhaps with a more open aspect and a larger, uninterrupted lawn for children to play on. There are few changes you can make in the garden that can have such a far-reaching effect on its entire visual perspective.

Retaining walls: If your new garden has an old, dilapidated retaining wall that would involve a lot of work to repair and improve, consider removing it entirely and forming a steep, grassy bank in its place. It will not take long for the grass to establish itself, and extra spring interest can be created by planting daffodil bulbs, together with polyanthus, all over the bank.

Hover mowers, as well as strimmers, are ideal for cutting grassy banks, but be sure to round off the top edge of your bank as otherwise the mower's blade will shave

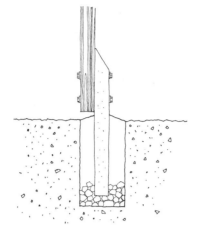

If your fence posts have rotted at the base, you must replace them. The use of a buried concrete spur saves rebuilding the entire fence.

Rickety, dilapidated fences can be expensive and time-consuming to replace, so instead use brackets and wood stain to improve them no end.

off the turf and create unattractive bare patches.

Steps: Steps can play an important visual role in the garden, as well as being essentially functional by nature. There are numerous different materials to choose from, not all of them necessarily that expensive. Sometimes, flights of steps can be made more attractive by laying extra paving slabs at the top and bottom, to create an 'entrance and exit' to the flight. Make these areas wider than the width of the steps themselves, so that plants in pots and tubs can be placed on them for added decoration.

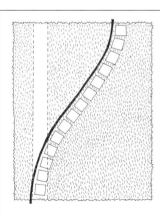

Moving a path

Changing the line and materials of a path can transform the entire garden.

Remove the old path and level the soil. If a new path in a lawn is needed, consider using stepping stones. These can meander attractively across the garden and are quicker and less expensive to install than a traditional path. Use a hosepipe to indicate the new path's position. Before finalizing the line and position of the path, view it carefully from all parts of the garden, as well as from upstairs windows.

Labour & time-saving ideas

Saving time and energy in a garden involves mechanizing tasks and ensuring that the garden's structure allows these to be used. Additionally, it helps to grow plants that need little attention; some plants are so gardener-friendly that they are both easy to grow *and* suppress the growth of weeds.

The key to time- and labour-efficient gardening is to strike the correct balance between using plants for natural effects and machines for undertaking essential tasks. Get the balance right, and you can spend more time relaxing in the comfort of your garden furniture.

Ground-cover plants

Many plants smother the soil's surface with attractive leaves and flowers and prevent the growth of weeds. Here are a few of them:

Dryas octopetala (mountain avens): Deep green leaves and white, saucer-shaped flowers.

Hosta fortunei 'Albopicta' (plantain lily): Pale green leaves, variegated buff yellow.

Lamium galeobdolon 'Florentinum' (previously known as *L. g.* 'Variegatum' and commonly as variegated yellow archangel): Leaves flushed silver, with attractive, yellow-coloured flowers.

Pulmonaria saccharata (Bethlehem sage): Green leaves spotted silvery-white; pink flowers that change to sky-blue.

Tiarella wherryi (false mitrewort): Pale green, ivy-shaped leaves.

Self-supporting herbaceous plants

Many herbaceous plants need support, but some are self-supporting and thereby reduce the attention required. They are ideal for planting in an 'island bed' on a lawn. Here are a few plants to consider:

Achillea millefolium (yarrow): White to cerise flowers in large, flattened heads.
Height: 60cm (2ft)
Plant: 30–38cm (12–15in)

Agapanthus 'Headbourne Hybrids' (African lily): Large, umbrella-like heads of violet-blue to pale blue flowers.
Height: 60–75cm (2–2½ft)
Plant: 38–45cm (15–18in) apart

Anemone × hybrida (Japanese anemone): White or pink flowers up to 7.5cm (3in) wide.
Height: 60–90cm (2–3ft)
Plant: 30–38cm (12–15in) apart

Camassia quamash (common camosh): White, purple or blue star-like flowers.
Height: 60–75cm (2–2½ft)
Plant: 15cm (6in)

Inula helenium (elecampane): Large, bright yellow, daisy-like flowers.
Height: 90cm–1.2m (3–4ft)
Plant: 38–45cm (15–18in) apart

Easy border edges

Use these tips to smarten up your border edges quickly and improve the look of the whole garden.

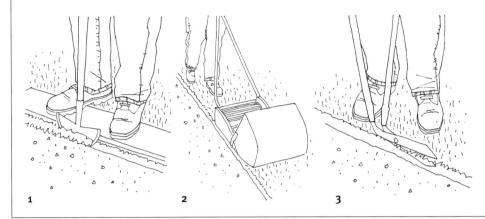

1
2
3

1) **Lay a plank alongside the edge you wish to cut. Use it both to stand on and to ensure a straight edge.**
2) **Use a roller-mower to overhang and mow right to the edge.**
3) **Tidy up any straggling grass with long-handled shears.**

Saving spring bulbs

Faded daffodils and tulips often spoil borders. Here's how to re-locate them without losing them.

1
2
3

1) **Dig the bulbs up after their flowers fade.**
2) **Bury the bulbs and their lower stems in a trench.**
3) **Allow the foliage to die down, then remove the bulbs, store in boxes and re-plant in late summer or early autumn.**

Getting mechanical and compatible

Lawns and their edges are the main areas where mechanization is needed.

Border edges: Use a half-moon edging-iron to cut edges. To trim grass at the edges, use long-arm edging-shears or a roller-edger.
Lawns abutting walls: Where lawns abut walls, use a strimmer or long-handled lawn shears. Strimmers cut grass quickly, but may damage decorative walls.
Stepping stones in lawns: Hover mowers are ideal for cutting lawns through which stepping-stone paths have been laid.

Paving stone edges: When a lawn is alongside a border, install a 30–45cm (12–18in) wide edging of paving. A hover-mower can then be used to cut the lawn's surface directly up to the paving.

Colour in the Garden

Colour is the most powerful natural force in any garden. It offers infinite variety, immensely evocative qualities and the ability to catch and hold the eye like no other element in the garden. In horticulture, colour has the finest natural medium of expression there is – plants.

Without plants, a garden is nothing; without colourful plants, it is incomplete. Plants offer every colour of the rainbow, every nuance of the spectrum, uniquely combining each infinitesimal hue and tone with countless different textures, shapes and sizes. From the brilliant blues, yellows and reds of spring annuals to the delicate, ghostly striations of winter barks, plants offer every colour and shade known to the human eye.

Given their limitless versatility, it is no wonder that colourful plants offer the greatest range of natural short cuts to beautiful gardens. Many of these plants are fully hardy throughout the year, others more delicate and ephemeral, but they all offer spellbinding powers of evocation. Plant a colourful garden, and very soon you will have a beautiful garden.

Colour contrasts and harmonies

Colour preference is an emotional choice which plants can normally fulfil admirably. However, scientifically, colour is classified according to its hue, value and intensity. For this reason, for gardeners it is a 'colour' wheel that offers the greatest practical assistance when choosing a particular colour and deciding whether it harmonizes or contrasts with another.

In the late seventeenth century Sir Isaac Newton invented a wheel formed of seven colours (red, orange, yellow, green, blue, indigo and violet). In the 1800s the American A. H. Munsell made a colour wheel of five main colours, with a further five intermediate colours between them. Nowadays, a simpler wheel formed of three basic colours (red, yellow and blue), with secondary colours where they overlap (green, orange and violet) is the one that is principally used. Such a wheel indicates complementary colours (those diametrically opposite) and ones that harmonize with each other (colours in adjacent segments).

Complementary colours are those with no common pigments, while harmonizing colours share the same pigments.

Dramatic or demure?

Whichever colour combinations you require in your garden, there are usually plants that can provide them.

A colour wheel can be used to show how plant colours may be selected to create dramatic features, or more subtle colour displays in your garden.

A colour wheel formed of three basic colours, with others created where they overlap, shows complementary and harmonizing colours. For example, yellow and violet, blue and orange, and red and green are complementary colours, whereas yellow harmonizes with green and orange, blue with green and violet, and red with orange and violet.

Shiny and matt surfaces

The surface texture of plants' leaves, stems and flowers dramatically influences the amount of light reflected from the plants in the garden and thus the perceived vibrancy of a border. A smooth surface reflects light at the same angle at which the rays hit it. This makes the light purer in colour than similar light reflected from a matt surface. So, for really bright, clear colours, select plants that have smooth, shiny surfaces.

Few sights in the garden are more beautiful than tulips in bloom alongside swathes of forget-me-not in spring and early summer.

The evening factor

The diminishing light of evening has a dramatic influence on the perception of colour. Clearly, all colours eventually disappear as the light fades, but some remain noticeable longer than others. Black is the first to disappear, then purple and deep red; yellow is one of the last to disappear into the gloom. Conversely, yellow is one of the first colours to become apparent each morning.

For this reason:
● Plant bright yellow conifers as focal points in gardens, or at the top or base of a flight of steps.
● Position columnar, yellow-foliaged conifers near garage entrances and at the ends of drives.
● Plant light-colour herbaceous plants at the end of a border, so that its extent is easily seen at twilight.

Simple summer-flowering bedding displays

Half-hardy annuals create a wealth of colour throughout summer and until the onset of frost in autumn. In the past, they were planted in massed and intricate designs, sometimes to form floral clocks or advertisements. Today, in small gardens they have many other uses.

Half-hardy annuals are ideal for:
- Creating attractive edgings to borders, paths and patios.
- As 'fillers' in borders that are a medley of herbaceous and bulbous plants, shrubs and small trees.
- In pots, tubs, hanging-baskets and windowboxes (see Chapter 4).
- As 'fillers' in newly-constructed rock gardens, where alpine plants are not yet established.
- As annual climbers to drench trellises in colour throughout summer.

Edging combinations

Colourful edgings to borders and patios create an immediate impact. Try the following 'edging' combinations.

White and blue: Plant *Lobularia maritima* 'Carpet of Snow' (previously known as *Alyssum maritimum*, and popularly as sweet alyssum) and *Lobelia erinus* 'Mrs Clibran Improved'.

Colour medley: *Impatiens* – choose individual flowers with several colours, as well as varieties with 'mixed' colours.

Bright, mixed colours: *Tagetes patula* 'Favourite Mixed' (French marigold).

Half-hardy annual climbers

Some of these are short-lived perennials, but in temperate climates are grown as half-hardy annuals. They are ideal for introducing quick, summer colour to trellises:

***Cobaea scandens* (cup-and-saucer vine):** Purple, bell-shaped flowers.
Height: 2.4–3m (8–10ft)
Plant: 45cm (18in) apart

***Eccremocarpus scaber* (Chilean glory flower):** Tubular, orange-scarlet flowers.
Height: 1.8–3m (6–10ft)
Plant: 45cm (18in) apart

Ipomoea tricolor* 'Heavenly Blue'** (sometimes known as ***I. rubro-caerulea, and popularly as morning glory): Large, blue, bell-shaped flowers.
Height: 2.4m (8ft)
Plant: 30cm (12in) apart

What are they?

Half-hardy annuals: Plants raised from seeds sown in early and mid-spring in gentle warmth in a greenhouse. When large enough to handle, half-hardy annual seedlings are transferred to wider spacings in seed-trays or boxes. Later, plants are slowly acclimatized to outdoor temperatures (known as hardening-off) and planted into gardens, once all risk of frost has passed.

***Maurandya scandens* 'Jewel Mixed'**
(previously known as ***Asarina scandens***,
and popularly as climbing snapdragon):
Violet, white, pink and deep blue flowers.
Height: 1.2–2.4m (4–8ft)
Plant: 10cm (4in) apart
***Tropaeolum peregrinum* (canary creeper):**
Irregular-shaped, yellow flowers. Can also
be grown as a hardy annual.
Height: 1.8–3m (6–10ft)
Plant: 75cm (2½ft) apart

Colourful leaves

Several half-hardy annuals have colourful
or variegated leaves, and when planted in
borders produce a dramatic display.
***Amaranthus tricolor* (Joseph's coat):** Green
leaves variegated crimson or scarlet and
overlaid with yellow and bronze.
Height: 60–90cm (2–3ft)
Plant: 30–45cm (1–1½ft) apart
***Bassia scoparia* 'Trichophylla'** (previously
known as ***Kochia scoparia* 'Trichophylla'**,
and popularly as summer cypress):
Profusion of narrow, pale green leaves that
turn coppery-crimson in autumn.
Height: 60–90cm (2–3ft)
Plant: 30–45cm (1–1½ft) apart
***Brassica* 'Northern Lights' (ornamental
cabbage):** White, pink, and purple forms.
Height: 23–30cm (9–12in)
Plant: 38–45cm (15–18in) apart
***Perilla frutescens* 'Nankinensis'** (often
known as ***P. f. crispa***): Bronze-purple,
deeply toothed leaves.
Height: 45–60cm (1½–2ft)
Plant: 30cm (1ft) apart
***Zea mays* (ornamental sweet corn):** Use a
form with variegated leaves.
Height: 90cm–1.5m (3–5ft)
Plant: 75cm (2½ft) apart

Colourful everlasting flowers

Several 'everlasting' flowers have a half-
hardy annual nature. These include:
***Celosia spicata* 'Flamingo Feather':** Rose
and deep-pink flowers.

***Craspedia globosa* 'Drumstick':** Silver
leaves and yellow flowers.
***Gnaphalium* 'Fairy Gold'** (also known as
***Helichrysum thianschanicum* 'Goldkind'**):
Silvery-grey leaves and double, yellow to
orange, flowers.
***Helichrysum monstrosum* 'Bright Bikini
Mixed':** Daisy-like flowers in many colours.
***Limonium sinuatum* 'Azure' (sea lavender):**
Blue flowers; but other varieties in yellow,
orange, pink, white, carmine.
***Moluccella laevis* (bells of Ireland):** Olive
to emerald-green bells.

**This exquisite border
features ageratums,
pelargoniums,
begonias and
fuchsias.**

Bright-faced hardy annuals

Hardy annuals are ideal for quickly and inexpensively drenching borders in colour throughout summer and often into early autumn. Some are low-growing, while others are tall and need support from twiggy sticks; insert them when plants are small, so that leaves and stems grow up and through them.

Colourful hardy annuals for rock gardens and border edges

Rock gardens, especially when new, have bare areas that can be brightened with hardy annuals. They can also be used to create low edgings to beds and borders. Here are a few plants to consider:

***Adonis aestivalis* (pheasant's eye):** Deep crimson flowers with black centres. Sow seeds 6mm (¼in) deep in spring.
Height: 25–30cm (10–12in)
Thin seedlings: 23cm (9in) apart

***Ionopsidium acaule* (violet cress):** Four-petalled, mauve or white flowers, tinged purple. Sow seeds 6mm (¼in) deep in spring.
Height: 5–7.5cm (2–3in)
Thin seedlings: 5–7.5cm (2–3in) apart; if seeds are sown thinly, they do not need to be thinned.

***Limnanthes douglasii* (poached egg plant):** White flowers with large, yellow centres. Sow seeds 3mm (⅛in) deep in spring.
Height: 15cm (6in)
Thin seedlings: 10cm (4in) apart

Linanthus androsaceus luteus (previously known as ***Gilia lutea***, and popularly as stardust): Brightly-coloured, star-shaped flowers in yellow, orange, red and pink. Sow seeds 6mm (¼in) deep in spring.
Height: 10–15cm (4–6in)
Thin seedlings: 10cm (4in) apart

A classic combination of hardy annuals in a border makes for stunning colour contrasts.

Nemophila menziesii (**baby blue eyes**): Sky-blue, saucer-shaped flowers. Sow seeds 6mm (¼in) deep.
Height: 23cm (9in)
Thin seedlings: 15cm (6in) apart

Bright-faced climbers

There are several hardy annuals that can be sown and grown where they are to flower. They are ideal as screening plants; a few have the bonus of scented flowers. Here are a couple to consider:

Lathyrus odoratus (**sweet pea**): Can be sown outdoors where it is to germinate and grow. Sow seeds in mid- or late spring, 12mm (½in) deep and about 15cm (6in) apart. These scented plants come in many different colours so are sure to add interest. Height: 1.2–3m (4–10ft)

Tropaeolum majus '**Climbing Mixed**' (**nasturtium**): Wealth of cerise, scarlet, orange, yellow or cream flowers. Sow seeds 12mm (½in) deep in spring.
Height: 1.8–2.4m (6–8ft)
Thin seedlings: 25–38cm (10–15in) apart

Biennials for all gardens

These resilient plants can be used on their own or mixed with other spring and early-summer flowering plants to create colourful displays.

Tall biennials

Two well-known biennials create magnificent displays and are ideal for cottage gardens and forming a peppered backdrop in borders.

Alcea rosea (previously known as *Althaea rosea*, and popularly as hollyhock): Single or double flowers, 10cm (4in) or more wide, in shades of pink, from mid-summer to early autumn. Height: 1.5–1.8m (5–6ft)
Plant: 60cm (2ft) apart

Digitalis purpurea (**foxglove**): Spires of bell-shaped flowers in red, through pink to purple, from early to late summer. Height: 90cm–1.5m (3–5ft) Plant: 45–60cm (1½–2ft)

Mixing and matching biennials

Tulips are ideal companions for biennials and can be used to create colourful displays in many different combinations.

Blue, scarlet and gold mixture: A carpet of pale blue forget-me-nots (*Myosotis*) and a mass of the gold-and-scarlet, single, early tulip 'Keizerskroon'. For a yellow, scarlet and gold combination, substitute the forget-me-nots for yellow violas.

Blue and gold mixture: Plant a golden wallflower, such as 'Golden Bedder', with the dark blue Darwin tulip 'La Tulipe Noire'. For extra shades of blue, add a few forget-me-nots (*Myosotis*).

Herbaceous plants

Herbaceous plants are generally easy to grow and will repay the initial effort involved in planting them. Once established, they create magnificent displays for three to five years before being dug up, divided and re-planted into new flowering positions.

The range of herbaceous plants is wide; some have spectacular flowers, while others develop coloured or variegated leaves.

Colour-theme borders

Borders with flowers and leaves sharing a particular colour theme were traditionally very popular. Extensive borders, often planted in pairs and positioned opposite one another, were colour-themed with gold-and-yellow, orange, blue, green, or silver-and-white plants. This style can still be created, but invariably on a smaller scale.

Gold-and-yellow:

Achillea filipendulina 'Coronation Gold' (fern-leaf achillea): Lemon-yellow flowers.
Alchemilla mollis (lady's mantle): Sulphur-yellow flowers and light green leaves.
Coreopsis verticillata: Bright yellow, star-like flowers and finely-divided leaves.

Doronicum × excelsum 'Harpur Crewe' (previously known as **D. plantagineum 'Excelsum'**, and popularly as leopard's bane): Single, golden-yellow, daisy-like flowers.
Phlomis fruticosa (Jerusalem sage): Tiered whorls of bright yellow flowers.
Rudbeckia fulgida (coneflower): Yellow to orange, 6.5cm (2¼in) wide flowers.
Solidago 'Goldenmosa' (golden rod): Tiny, yellow flowers in feathery plumes.
Trollius × cultorum (globe flower): Yellow to orange, large, globe-shaped flowers.

Blue and mauve:

Aconitum napellus (monkshood): Hooded, deep blue flowers. Several excellent varieties.
Anchusa azurea (alkanet): Bright blue, forget-me-not-like flowers in lax heads.
Aster amellus 'King George' (Italian starwort): Large, daisy-like, blue-violet flowers with golden-yellow centres.
Aster × frikartii: Large, daisy-like blue flowers with orange centres.
Campanula lactiflora (milky bellflower): Lavender-blue, bell-like flowers.
Chelone obliqua (turtle-head): Deep rose, snapdragon-like flowers borne in clusters.
Echinops ritro (globe thistle): Round, steel-blue flowers up to 5cm (2in) wide.

What are they?

Herbaceous perennials: Plants that each spring develop fresh shoots which grow and bear flowers before the onset of frost in autumn or early winter. Herbaceous borders, however, are not just filled with these plants, but bulbous and tuberous-rooted types as well. Additionally, they often contain a few border plants that retain their leaves throughout much of winter. These include *Stachys byzantina* (lamb's tongue) and bergenias.

Incarvillea mairei (**trumpet flower**):
Trumpet-like, pinkish-purple flowers.
Liatris spicata (**blazing star**): Pinkish-purple flowers in paint-brush heads.
Salvia × superba (**long-branched sage**):
Tall, violet-purple spires.
Tradescantia × andersoniana **'Isis'**
(**spiderwort**): Purple-blue flowers.

Pink and red:

Aster novi-belgii **'Orlando'** (**Michaelmas daisy**): Semi-double pink flowers.
Crocosmia masonorum **'Vulcan'**
(**montbretia**): Clusters of orange-red, trumpet-like flowers.
Dicentra spectabilis (**bleeding heart**):
Pendulous, rose-red, heart-shaped flowers.
Euphorbia griffithii **'Fireglow'**: Orange-red bracts clustered at the tops of stems.
Hemerocallis **'Pink Damask'** (**day lily**): Large, warm-pink flowers with yellow throats.
Kniphofia (**torch lily**): Several species and varieties with red flowers in poker-like heads.
Schizostylis coccinea **'Major'**: Rich, vivid-crimson flowers.

Silver and white:

Anaphalis triplinervis (**pearly everlasting**):
White flowers and leaves.
Artemisia ludoviciana (**white sage**): White leaves and silvery-white flowers.
Leucanthemum × vulgare (previously known as *Chrysanthemum maximum*, and popularly as Shasta daisy): Large, white, daisy-like flowers.
Gypsophila paniculata (**baby's breath**):
Massed white flowers in lax, clustered heads.
Onopordum acanthium (**ornamental thistle**): Jaggedly-lobed, silvery-grey leaves.
Romneya coulteri (**tree poppy**): Large, white flowers with bright golden centres.
Stachys byzantina (**lamb's tongue**): Oval leaves smothered in silvery-white hairs.

A classic mixed border in mid-summer, featuring a rich interplanting of rudbeckia, lavender, snapdragons and salvia, amongst others.

Wall and trellis brighteners

Climbers come from a medley of plant types and are excellent for decorating walls, pergolas and trellises: some are evergreen with variegated leaves, a few are deciduous and reveal richly-coloured leaves in autumn, while many have magnificent flowers. Several climbers offer the bonus of scent. Whichever ones you select for your garden, they will create an impressive display.

Evergreen climbers

***Hedera canariensis* 'Gloire de Marengo' (variegated Canary Island ivy):** Large, thick and leathery leaves, deep green at their centres, merging into silvery-grey and with creamy-white edges.
Height: 4.5–6m (15–20ft)
Self-clinging on walls, but also can be grown on a trellis.

***Hedera colchica* 'Dentata Variegata' (variegated Persian ivy):** Large, thick, leathery, bright green leaves edged in creamy-white.
Height: 6–7.5m (20–25ft)
Self-clinging on walls, but can also be grown on a trellis.

***Hedera colchica* 'Sulphur Heart':** Large, leathery, broadly oval, deep green leaves splashed and irregularly streaked in yellow.
Height: 5.4–6m (18–20ft)
Self-clinging on walls, but can also be grown on a trellis.

***Lonicera japonica* 'Aureoreticulata' (variegated Japanese honeysuckle):** Oval, light green leaves with midribs and veins lined in yellow. In cold areas it is semi-evergreen.
Height: 1.2–2.4m (4–8ft)
Requires a trellis; can also be planted to sprawl through sage and variegated apple mint.

Deciduous climbers

***Actinidia kolomikta* (Kolomikta vine):** Dark green, slightly heart-shaped leaves up to 15cm (6in) long, marked at their tips in white or pink.
Height: 2.4–3.6m (8–12ft)
Requires support.

***Humulus lupulus* 'Aureus' (golden-leaved hop):** Fast-growing herbaceous climber with scrambling stems packed with hop-like, bright yellowish-green leaves. In autumn, stems die down to soil-level.
Height: 1.8–3m (8–10ft)
Requires an arch or trellis.

***Jasminum officinale* 'Aureum':** Hardy, deciduous, twining climber with leaves blotched creamy-yellow.
Height: 2.4–3.6m (8–12ft)
Requires a trellis.

***Parthenocissus henryana* (Chinese Virginia creeper):** Dark green, three- to five-lobed leaves variegated pink and white along the veins and midrib. In autumn, the variegations become even more defined and the green parts assume a brilliant red.
Height: 6–7.5m (20–25ft)
Self-clinging on walls.

***Parthenocissus tricuspidata* (Boston ivy):** Very vigorous, with variably-shaped leaves that assume rich colours in autumn. Only suitable for large walls.

Opposite: Sunflowers are not actually climbers, but their height and large, brilliant flower heads mean that they will provide a stunning counterpoint to any wall, trellis or other tall garden feature.

Height: 9–12m (30–40ft)
Self-clinging on walls.
Vitis coignetiae **(crimson glory vine):** Very
vigorous, with rounded but lobed, mid-
green leaves. In autumn they assume rich
colours. Only suitable for large walls.
Height: 12m (40ft) – or more
Best when allowed to ramble into trees;
alternatively, on large pergolas.

Glorious flowers

Ceanothus thrysiflorus repens
(Californian lilac): Evergreen wall
shrub, with light blue flowers.
Height: 1.2–1.5m (4–5ft)
Provide a low trellis, against which it
can be trained and loosely tied.
Clematis montana **(mountain clematis):**
Deciduous, with 5cm (2in) white or pink
flowers. Several superb varieties.
Height: 5.4–7.5m (18–25ft)
Requires a trellis.
Clematis – large-flowered hybrids:
Deciduous, with large flowers in a range
of colours.
Height: 1.2–4.5m (4–15ft) – range
Requires a trellis.
Hydrangea petiolaris **(Japanese climbing
hydrangea):** Deciduous and rambling,
with creamy-white flower heads.
Height: 4.5–9m (15–30ft)
Self-clinging on walls, but benefits from
a trellis.
Jasminum nudiflorum **(winter-flowering
jasmine):** Deciduous wall shrub, with bright
yellow flowers from autumn to spring.
Height: 1.2–1.8m (4–6ft)
Requires a trellis to which it can be
secured.
Jasminum officinale **(common jasmine):**
Deciduous, with lax clusters of white flowers.
Height: 6–7.5m (20–25ft)
Requires a trellis.
Lonicera japonica **(Japanese honeysuckle):**
Evergreen, with white to pale yellow
flowers.
Height: 4.5–7.5m (15–25ft)
Requires a trellis, arch or pergola.

Colourful shrubs and trees for all seasons

The range of shrubs and trees is wide and while they create a wealth of flowers in spring, summer and winter, others have colourful stems and bark that help to bring added interest to gardens, especially during winter. Some trees and shrubs work particularly well when planted in combination with other plants. Here are some exciting combinations.

Flowers for spring

Amelanchier lamarckii **(snowy mespilus):** Deciduous shrub or small tree with clouds of star-shaped, pure white flowers, with the bonus of coloured leaves in autumn. Plant a sea of golden daffodils around it.
Height: 4.5–7.5m (15–25ft)
Spread: 3.6–6m (12–20ft)

Forsythia × intermedia **(golden bells):** Deciduous shrub with clusters of golden-yellow flowers. For a completely yellow theme, plant golden daffodils around it.
Height: 1.8–2.4m (6–8ft)
Spread: 1.5–2.1m (5–7ft)

Magnolia stellata **(star magnolia):** Deciduous shrub with star-shaped, 10cm (4in) wide, white flowers. Plant small, blue-flowered bulbs around it.
Height: 2.4–3m (8–10ft)
Spread: 2.4–3m (8–10ft)

Spiraea **'Arguta'** (previously known as *Spiraea × arguta*, and popularly as bridal wreath): Deciduous shrub that reveals massed clusters of small, white flowers. Plant a medley of the blue-flowered *Scilla siberica* and *S. tubergeniana* (but now correctly known as *S. mischtschenkoana*), snowdrops and the yellow-flowered winter aconite around it.
Height: 1.8–2.4m (6–8ft)
Spread: 1.5–2.1m (5–7ft)

Ulex europaeus **'Plenus' (double-flowered gorse):** Spiny, evergreen with golden-yellow, pea-shaped flowers. It is especially attractive in a country setting and when set alongside a post-and-rail fence.
Height: 1.5–2.1m (5–7ft)
Spread: 1.5–2.1m (5–7ft)

Flowers for summer

Buddleja alternifolia: Deciduous shrub, with cascading stems bearing lavender-blue flowers. It is best planted in a lawn, rather

---

Other spring-flowering shrubs and trees

Berberis darwinii (Darwin's berberis)
Chaenomeles speciosa (Japanese quince)
Choisya ternata (Mexican orange bush)
Magnolia liliiflora 'Nigra'
Prunus 'Accolade'
Prunus padus 'Watereri' (bird cherry)
Prunus × subhirtella 'Pendula Rosea' (weeping spring cherry)

than a border, where it tends to dominate.
Height: 3–4.5m (10–15ft)
Spread: 3–4.5m (10–15ft)

Cytisus × praecox (Warminster broom):
Deciduous shrub with arching stems bearing creamy-white, pea-shaped flowers. When planted with the flowering currant *Ribes sanguineum* and a forsythia it creates an attractive group.
Height: 1.5–1.8m (5–6ft)
Spread: 1.5–1.8, (5–6ft)

Hibiscus syriacus (shrubby mallow):
Deciduous shrub with large, 7.5cm (3in) wide flowers. Varieties include 'Blue Bird' (violet-blue and now known as *H. s.* 'Oiseau Bleu'), 'Woodbridge' (rose-pink) and 'Red Heart' (white with bright red centres).
Height: 1.8–3m (8–10ft)
Spread: 1.2–1.8m (4–6ft)

Hypericum 'Hidcote' (rose of Sharon):
Almost evergreen shrub, with large, saucer-like, golden-yellow flowers up to 7.5cm (3in) wide. It is ideal for covering large, bare banks.
Height: 90cm–1.5m (3–5ft)
Spread: 1.5–2.1m (5–7ft)

Laburnum × watereri 'Vossii' (golden rain tree): Deciduous tree with golden-yellow, pea-shaped flowers in pendulous clusters up to 60cm (2ft) long.

Shrubs and trees bring height and form to a garden, but it is the added bonuses of beautiful blossom and striking foliage that really make the difference. Here, a *Liquidambar stryaciflua* 'Lane Roberts' shows off its beautifully-coloured autumn leaves.

Other summer-flowering shrubs and trees

Caryopteris × clandonensis
Ceanothus 'Gloire de Versailles' (Californian lilac)
Cistus × lusitanicus (sun rose)
Eucryphia × nymansensis
Genista aetnensis (Mt. Etna broom)
Genista cinerea
Genista hispanica (Spanish broom)
Hebe 'Autumn Glory' (shrubby veronica)

Hydrangea arborescens (hills of snow)
Kalmia latifolia (calico bush)
Kerria japonica 'Pleniflora' (bachelor's buttons)
Kolkwitzia amabilis (beauty bush)
Romneya coulteri trichocalyx (Californian tree poppy)
Weigela Hybrids

Many trees and shrubs offer defining architectural form year-round in the garden. Add out-of-season colour as well, and the effects can be stunning.

Philadelphus 'Avalanche' (mock orange): Deciduous, with arching branches bearing sweetly-scented white, cup-shaped flowers. There are several excellent hybrids.
Height: 90cm–1.5m (3–5ft)
Spread: 1.2–1.8m (4–6ft)

Potentilla fruticosa (shrubby cinquefoil): Deciduous shrub bearing masses of buttercup-yellow flowers, each about 2.5cm (1in) wide. As well as being planted in a shrub border, it can be formed into a hedge.
Height: 1–1.2m (3–4ft)
Spread: 1–1.2m (3–4ft)

Syringa pubescens microphylla 'Superba': Deciduous shrub, with rose-pink flowers.
Height: 1.8–2.4m (6–8ft)
Spread: 1.8–2.1m (6–7ft)

Flowers for winter

Cornus mas (cornelian cherry): Deciduous, twiggy shrub that reveals golden-yellow flowers in small clusters on naked stems.
Height: 2.4–3.6m (8–12ft)
Spread: 1.8–3m (6–10ft)

Daphne mezereum (mezereon): Deciduous shrub with fragrant, purple-red flowers that cluster tightly on the stems. Also a white-flowered form.
Height: 90cm–1.5m (3–5ft)
Spread: 60–90cm (2–3ft)

Hamamelis mollis (Chinese witch hazel): Deciduous shrub or small tree with spreading branches bearing clusters of golden-yellow, spider-like flowers along naked branches. It associates with sweet

Other trees and shrubs with colourful bark and stems

Acer davidii (snakebark maple)
Acer pensylvanicum (moosebark maple)
Arbutus andrachne (Grecian strawberry tree)
Betula albosinensis septentrionalis
Betula ermanii (Erman's birch)
Betula papyrifera (canoe birch)
Cornus alba (red-barked dogwood)
Phyllostachys nigra (black-stemmed bamboo)

Other winter-flowering shrubs and trees

Chimonanthus praecox (winter sweet)
Daphne odora (winter daphne)
Erica carnea (erica)
Erica × darleyensis (erica)
Viburnum × bodnantense
Viburnum farreri

box (*Sarcococca confusa*) and a low, golden-leaved form of the evergreen *Euonymus japonicus*.
Height: 1.8–3m (6–10ft)
Spread: 2.1–3m (7–10ft)
***Mahonia × media* 'Charity':** Evergreen shrub with leathery, spine-toothed leaves formed of many leaflets, and deep lemon-yellow flowers in long, upright spires.
Height: 1.8–2.4m (6–8ft)
Spread: 1.5–2.1m (5–7ft)
***Viburnum tinus* (laurustinus):** Evergreen shrub with white flowers, pink in bud.
Height: 2.1–2.7m (7–9ft)
Spread: 1.5–2.1m (5–7ft)

Colourful barks and stems

Throughout the year, and especially in winter, trees and shrub with coloured bark or stems create unfailing colour, whatever the weather. Position them where the sun's rays strike and enhance them.
***Acer griseum* (Chinese paperbark maple):** Slow-growing deciduous tree displaying buff-coloured bark that peels to reveal orange-brown under bark.
Height: 3.6–4.5m (12–15ft)
Spread: 2.4–3m (8–10ft)
***Arbutus × andrachnoides*:** Evergreen tree that reveals attractive cinnamon-red bark.
Height: 3–4.5m (10–15ft)
Spread: 2.1–2.7m (7–9ft)
***Betula utilis* 'Jacquemontii':** Deciduous tree, bearing peeling bark, usually white,

but light pinkish-brown and ochre-cream forms are known.
Height: 6–9m (20–30ft)
Spread: 3–4.5m (10–15ft)
***Calocedrus decurrens* (incense cedar):** Slow-growing, evergreen conifer with scaly, rough-textured, reddish-brown bark.
Height: 6–7.5m (20–25ft)
Spread: 2.4–3.6m (8–12ft)
***Cornus stolonifera* 'Flaviramea' (dogwood):** Deciduous, suckering, spreading shrub with bright greenish-yellow young stems in winter. To encourage their yearly production, cut back all shoots to 5–7.5cm (2–3in) of soil-level in spring.
Height: 1.8–2.4m (6–8ft)
Spread: 2.1–3m (7–10ft)

Winter is a time when the trunks and stems of many trees and shrubs come into their own, compensating for a lack of colour and vibrancy elsewhere in the garden. *Acer Pensylvanicum* 'Erythrocladum' exhibits beautifully-coloured bark throughout the year, and is especially noticeable during winter.

Colourful conifers

Conifers are some of the most garden-worthy of all plants; they are usually hardy, colourful and come in a wide range of shapes and sizes. Some are ideal for cloaking unsightly features, others just great brighteners.

Upright conifers

Yellow and gold:

Chamaecyparis lawsoniana 'Lutea': Feathery sprays of golden-yellow leaves.
Height: 9m (30ft)
Width: 1.5–1.8m (5–6ft)
Cupressus macrocarpa 'Goldcrest': Feathery, rich yellow, scale-like foliage.
Height: 4.5–7.5m (15–25ft)
Width: 1.5–1.8m (5–6ft)
Juniperus chinensis 'Aurea': Tall and slender, slow-growing conifer with golden foliage.
Height: 4.5–6m (15–20ft)
Width: 1–1.5m (3–5ft)

Blue:

Chamaecyparis lawsoniana 'Columnaris Glauca': Narrow, columnar with glaucous foliage blended with blue and green.
Height: 3–3.6m (10–12ft)
Width: 1–1.2m (3–4ft)
Chamaecyparis lawsoniana 'Pembury Blue': Initially bush-shaped, but later columnar, with silvery-blue foliage.
Height: 2.4–3m (8–10ft)
Width: 1.2–1.5m (4–5ft)
Cupressus glabra 'Pyramidalis': Eventually large, with a conical habit densely covered with blue-grey foliage.
Height: 4–6m (13–20ft)
Width: 1.8–2.4m (6–8ft)

Ground-hugging conifers

Yellow and gold:

Juniperus × pfitzeriana 'Gold Sovereign': Brilliant golden-yellow foliage on spreading and cascading stems.
Height: 45–50cm (18–20in)
Spread: 75–90cm (2½–3ft)
Juniperus 'Pfitzeriana Aurea': Low-growing and irregularly outlined, with golden-yellow foliage.
Height: 90cm–1.2m (3–4ft)
Spread: 1.2–1.5m (4–5ft)

Blue:

Juniperus horizontalis 'Wiltonii': Ground-hugging, with long branches bearing glaucous, silvery-blue foliage.
Height: 10–15cm (4–6in)
Width: 90cm–1m (3–3¼ft)
Juniperus squamata 'Blue Star': Prostrate, with arching and ascending branches bearing needle-like, bright steel-blue foliage.
Height: 30–45cm (12–18in)
Width: 45–60cm (1½–2ft)

Mixing and matching conifers

Prostrate and dwarf conifers are ideal companions for heaths and heathers with coloured foliage, creating contrasts and harmonies throughout the year.

Plant *Juniperus squamata* 'Blue Star' in a sea of the yellow-foliaged *Erica carnea* 'Foxhollow'.

Plant green foliaged conifers with the golden-yellow foliage *Calluna vulgaris* 'Golden Feather'.

Green and grey:

Juniperus communis 'Hornibrookii': Foliage first green, later bronze.
Height: 25–30cm (10–12in)
Spread: 1.2–1.5m (4–5ft)
Juniperus sabina 'Tamariscifolia': Dense and prostrate, with feathery, bright green foliage, greyish-green when young.
Height: 25–30cm (10–12in)
Spread: 1–1.5m (3–5ft)

Bun-shaped and cone-like conifers

Yellow and gold:

Chamaecyparis lawsoniana 'Minima Aurea': Rounded, slightly conical, slow-growing, with vertical sprays of bright yellow foliage.
Height: 50–60cm (20–24in)
Width: 60–75cm (2–2½ft)
Chamaecyparis pisifera 'Filifera Aurea': Slow-growing, with a cone-like outline and golden, thread-like foliage.
Height: 90cm–1.8m (3–6ft)
Width: 90cm–1.5m (3–5ft)

Blue:

Abies lasiocarpa 'Arizonica Compacta': Slow-growing, broadly pyramidal conifer with blue-grey leaves.
Height: 60–90cm (2–3ft)
Spread: 50–60cm (20–24in)
Chamaecyparis pisifera 'Boulevard': Broadly pyramidal, with silvery-blue foliage.
Height: 1–1.2m (3–4ft)
Spread: 1–1.2m (3–4ft)

Green and grey:

Abies balsamea 'Hudsonia': Dense, compact with grey leaves that turn mid-green as they mature during summer.
Height: 30–45cm (1–1½ft)
Spread: 45–60cm (1½–2ft)
Picea glauca albertina 'Conica': Conical, with soft grass-green foliage.
Height: 75cm–1.2m (2½–4ft)
Spread: 60–90cm (2–3ft)
Tsuga canadensis 'Jeddeloh': Semi-prostrate, with gracefully drooping branches bearing light, fresh green foliage.
Height: 30–45cm (1–1½ft)
Spread: 45–60cm (1½ft–2ft)

This sloping bed of mixed conifers, photographed in mid-winter sunshine, provides colour, architectural form and good screening all at the same time.

Livening Up Your Garden

If you are short of time and do not want to spend a fortune on completely re-modelling your garden, you must seek ways to enrich and enliven what you already have. By growing a few extra plants in pots, hanging-baskets and tubs on a patio, or by covering a previously bland wall in a climber that produces beautiful summer flowers or autumn-tinted leaves, you will soon transform your garden out of the ordinary and into a place that will put a smile on your face every time you look at it. Choose plants with rich and unusual fragrances – from vanilla to orange, curry to turpentine – or decorative natural features that create soothing sounds, and you will improve your garden's satisfaction rating still further.

Enriching gardens with memories

One way to liven up patios and gardens is to use plants that evoke memories of important events from earlier years, such as weddings, honeymoons, birthdays and special holidays. Many plants – such as Californian poppies native to the warm west coast of North America or fields of sunflowers seen in France – are able to evoke memories through their flowers or leaves. Lilac blossom, with its distinctive fragrance, strong colour and form, has traditionally been used in wedding bouquets, so planting a lilac tree in your garden might both enliven it and stir rich memories of a happy wedding day. For recollections of a holiday in India (or maybe just the Tandoori restaurant down the road!), try the curry plant, *Helichrysum italicum* (but still better known as *H. angustifolium*). Although it is not actually an Asian plant, it has a curry-like bouquet.

Touching times

We expect colour, sound and scent to enrich gardens, but the sensation of touch is also important in the garden. Getting to know soft-textured plants through touch is a form of solace and comfort, in much the same way as stroking a dog or cat can reduce tension and lower blood pressure. The range of plants that are pleasant to the touch is wide and includes:

Stachys: The lamb's tongue (*Stachys byzantium*, but still known as *S. lanata* or *S. olympica*) has soft, woolly and hairy leaves.

Phlomis: The Jerusalem sage (*Phlomis fruiticosa*) has wedge-shaped, woolly and grey-green leaves, with whorls of yellow flowers during early and mid-summer.

Clematis: The soft, umbrella-like, silvery heads of *Clematis vitalba* (old man's beard) appear in autumn and remain through much of winter.

Cortaderia: The large, plume-like flower heads of *Cortaderia selloana* (pampas grass) are dramatic both to the hand and the eye.

This garden has been carefully planned and planted to create an evocative atmosphere in the evening. The combination of fragrant plants, painted garden furniture, candles and ornaments creates an ambience akin to that of an outside room.

Opposite: The height and majesty of this large, pedestal-mounted urn containing a spiky agave would create an instant distraction in any garden.

Patios, courtyards and terraces – walls and floors

Each of these areas is different, but all have floors and either surrounding walls or walls close by. Floors generally need enlivening. Walls not only offer the opportunity to grow flowering and attractively foliaged climbers, but to display plants in hanging-baskets.

Above: The richness of planting on display here disguises what is otherwise a bland and uninteresting courtyard. Beautiful flowers and leaves will always draw the eye away from ugly brickwork and drainpipes.

A wall's colour dramatically influences the planting display in front of it, so here are a variety of quick and easy ways to colour-harmonize and contrast plants against white, red, and grey backgrounds – during both spring and summer.

White walls

Select mainly yellow, gold, red and green flowers, as well as plants with light or medium-green leaves.

Spring displays:

Golden-yellow wallflowers and light blue forget-me-nots.
● Red wallflowers and white, double-flowered daisies.
● A combination of red- and blue-flowered hyacinths.

Summer displays:

● Red or deep pink regal pelargoniums.
● Red or deep pink trailing geraniums (pelargoniums).

- Calceolarias; for a mixture of yellow, scarlet, rich red and copper-orange choose the variety 'Sunset Mixed'.
- Compact and low, double-flowered forms of French marigolds (tagetes), in reddish-mahogany, orange or yellow.
- Red or pink petunias; use pendulous types at the fronts of containers.
- Position yellow, orange or scarlet-flowered forms of trailing nasturtiums (*Tropaeolum*) at the fronts of windowboxes and wall-baskets.

Grey stone walls

Choose plants with deep purple, deep blue, pink and red flowers.

Spring displays:
- Red wallflowers and double-flowered pink daisies (*Bellis perennis*).
- Rich cherry-red, double-flowered daisies, such as *Bellis perennis* 'Kito'.
- Deep blue forget-me-nots (*Myosotis*) and single or double-flowered pink tulips.
- A combination of pink and blue hyacinths.
- Polyanthus: choose either single-colour plants, or a strain predominantly formed of flowers in blue, pink and red.

Summer displays:
Choose blue, purple, deep pink and red varieties of petunias. Use trailing varieties at the fronts of windowboxes and wall-baskets. Plant a combination of deep blue trailing lobelia and scarlet regal pelargoniums.
- Choose red or deep pink cascading fuchsias.
- Plant red or scarlet trailing varieties of nasturtiums at the front edges and sides of windowboxes.
- Choose a duo of bright crimson and yellow-flowered tuberous begonias. There are also red- and yellow-flowered pendulous forms.

Red brick walls

Select mainly white, soft blue, silver and lemon flowers.

Spring displays:
- Blue-flowered forget-me-nots (*Myosotis*) and white hyacinths.
- A combination of bronze and cream wallflowers, and pink and white daisies (*Bellis*).

Summer displays:
- Soft blue stocks and an edging of white sweet alyssum (*Lobularia maritima*, but still better known as *Alyssum maritimum*). The silver-leaved *Senecio cineraria* 'White Diamond' and blue-flowered stocks.

Below: A scruffy floor will always badly let down a garden, so it is important to lay attractive stones and patterns. This is particularly important in the case of patios, courtyards and terraces. Here are some ideas.

Lively patterns for paths, patios, courtyards and terraces

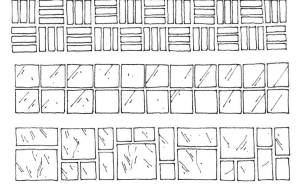
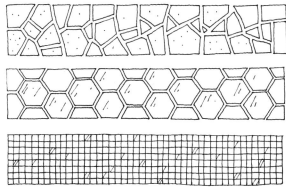

Livening up windowboxes

Scented windowboxes are a tonic throughout the year. Even winter can be enriched with fragrances from miniature and slow-growing conifers. Here is how to create memorable scents in windowboxes.

Scented winter windowboxes

Many miniature and slow-growing conifers can be put in windowboxes to create a scented display throughout the year, but this will be especially appreciated in winter when the range of scented flowers is limited. These conifers emit a bouquet when their foliage is bruised or stroked. Because close proximity to the aromatic foliage is essential, these conifers are best used in windowboxes for ground-floor windows, as well as windows on balconies. Eventually, these conifers will outgrow a windowbox and have to be moved to a rock garden or another part of the garden.
***Chamaecyparis lawsoniana* 'Elwoodii':** resin and parsley fragrance.

***Chamaecyparis lawsoniana* 'Elwood's Gold':** resin and parsley fragrance.
***Chamaecyparis lawsoniana* 'Pygmaea Argentea':** resin and parsley fragrance.
***Chamaecyparis obtusa* 'Nana':** warm and sweet bouquet.
***Chamaecyparis obtusa* 'Nana Aurea':** warm and sweet bouquet.
***Chamaecyparis obtusa* 'Pygmaea':** warm and sweet bouquet.
***Chamaecyparis pisifera* 'Boulevard':** resin-like fragrance.
***Juniperus communis* 'Compressa':** apple-like fragrance.

Small late-winter and spring-flowering scented bulbs for windowboxes

These, like the conifers in winter-fragrant windowboxes, need close examination. But this time they can be used for wind-sheltered first-floor windows as well as at ground level.

Small, scented bulbs are especially appreciated where first-floor bedrooms have sash-type windows, which readily enable the flowers to be admired and allow the fragrances to waft indoors.
Crocus chrysanthus: honey-like redolence during late winter and early spring.
Crocus longiflorus: primrose-like bouquet during early and mid-winter.
Crocus versicolor (also known as ***C. fragrans***): primrose-like bouquet during early spring.
Galanthus allenii: almond-like scent in spring.
Galanthus elwesii: violet-like scent from late winter to early spring.

Hanging-baskets bursting with vibrantly coloured and scented flowers create spectacular features throughout summer. Position them slightly to one side of a window, so that strong wind does not blow them against the glass. A combination of windowboxes and hanging-baskets creates an un-forgettable display.

Galanthus nivalis (**common snowdrop**): moss-like redolence from mid-winter into spring.

Iris danfordiae: honey-like and sweet, from mid- to late winter.

Plants for scented summer-flowering windowboxes

Heliotropium arborescens (**heliotrope/cherry pie**): sweet, heavy, fruity and resembling a cherry pie.

Laurentia axillaris ‘**Stars' Series**’: soft and gentle fragrance.

Matthiola incana ‘**Cinderella Antique Pink**’ (**stock**): Delicious clove-like fragrance.

Nicotiana alata (**tobacco plant**): very sweet and slightly heady.

Reseda odorata (**mignonette**): heady, sweet and very distinctive.

Viola × *wittrockiana* ‘**Singing the Blues**’: pervading sweetness.

Biennials for fragrance

Biennial plants are an inexpensive way to brighten beds alongside walls and under windowboxes. They are planted in late summer or early autumn, and during the following spring and early to mid-summer drench gardens with rich fragrances.

Dianthus barbatus (**sweet william**): Sweetly fragrant, single or double flowers during early and mid-summer; variously coloured, from white to red, or marked in other colours.

Erysimum × *allionii* (**Siberian wallflower**) and *E. cheiri* (**wallflower**): sweetly-scented, in a colour range that includes orange, white, yellow, scarlet, crimson and purple.

Scented flowering shrubs for tubs

These are relatively mobile plants and can be positioned where their fragrances are most welcome, perhaps near entrances. Choose a warm patio setting for the oleander, which is a Mediterranean plant.

A bulb-planter packed with spring-flowering crocuses creates a colourful and fragrant feature on a patio. The bulbs are planted in early autumn.

Be prepared to move these shrubs to a garden setting when they become too large for the container.

Lavandula angustifolia (**lavender**): Greyish-blue flowers from mid-summer to autumn.

Nerium oleander (**oleander**): Tender evergreen shrub, with single and double flowers in white, cream, pink and red, sweet and almond-scented flowers during mid- and late summer. All parts of this plant are poisonous.

Bulb planters for patio scent

Bulb planters resemble large pots and are also known as multiple planters or strawberry pots. They feature cupped planting pockets in their sides and are ideal containers for spring-flowering bulbs. They are available in ornate plastic, fibreglass and terracotta.

The honey-like, sweet, miniature and bulbous *Crocus chrysanthus* creates a spectacular display, with its rich golden-yellow flowers that appear during late winter and early spring. There are also forms in other colours.

When planting these bulbs in autumn, check that drainage holes in the base are open. Cover these with pieces of broken clay pots (crocks), then fill to level with the lowest cup with well-drained, loam-based compost. Put two or three bulbs in the hole and ensure they are well-covered with compost. Fill with further compost and continue to plant the bulbs. At the top, plant bulbs 5cm (2in) apart. Water the compost and place in a sheltered corner.

Doorways & entrances

Any entrance will be enlivened by climbers trailing around it or by plants in containers positioned on either side. Some containers have a formal nature and are best used beside buildings with cleaner, more clinical lines. Others have a more informal style that immediately harmonizes with older properties. They come in all kinds of materials:

Fibreglass: This is a modern synthetic material that comes in a variety of forms; it can take on the most intricate of patterns and designs. Indeed, it can be given the appearance of wood or even antique lead. Containers made out of fibreglass include windowboxes, troughs and urns.

Lead windowboxes and troughs: Containers made out of lead are expensive and have an aged appearance, but they are very attractive.

Plastic: Increasingly, containers of all types are made from plastic, including urns, troughs, planters, tubs and windowboxes.

They usually have a clinical nature and are best reserved for modern settings.

Reconstituted stone: Used to construct stone-like containers such as troughs and urns. These are heavy, with an attractive stone-like and aged appearance. Some are vase-shaped, while others come wide and shallow. Those positioned near entrances are best placed on the ground or on low pedestals.

Wooden tubs: These are usually barrels cut in half. Tubs with untreated surfaces have a rustic appearance, while those that have been smoothed and varnished look modern.

This classically decorated entrance is both beautiful and welcoming. It is also relatively easy to manage: many of the plants have been placed in containers or grown in hanging-baskets. Regularly removing dead flowers helps to prolong the display.

Wooden troughs: Those constructed from roughly-cut timber have a rustic nature, while troughs formed of planed timber are more clinical and modern.

Wooden Versailles planters: These have an old design and are best suited to perennial plants such as clipped box or agapanthus (African lily).

Prefabricated wooden or metal arches

These can be bought ready for assembly around entrances to create supports for flowering climbers. Do not use too-vigorous climbers, as they can block out light which can result in a gloomy entrance. For the same reason, do not use evergreen climbers such as large-leaved ivies, which as well as casting continual shade on the front door will certainly harbour spiders! Several clematis, however, have a more delicate nature, and good ones to use include:

Clematis flammula: Deciduous and bushy, up to 3m (10ft) high and eventually creating a tangle of stems at its top. Sweetly-scented, pure-white flowers appear from late summer to mid-autumn.

Clematis macropetala: Slender and deciduous, growing to about 4.5m (15ft) high, with light and dark blue, nodding, bell-shaped flowers up to 7.5cm (3in) wide during late spring and early summer.

Clematis tangutica: Deciduous, up to about 4.5cm (15ft) high, with yellow, lantern-shaped flowers about 5cm (2in) wide from late summer to mid-autumn. It has the bonus of silvery seed heads. If possible, add small trellises on either side of the door, so that it can also scramble over them.

Clematis – Large-flowered hybrids: There are many to choose from; most with single-flowers, others double.

'Ernest Markham': Single, velvety-red flowers mid-summer to autumn.

'Jackmanii Superba': Single, dark violet-purple flowers mid-summer to autumn.

Cottage garden climbers

Few climbers have a more rustic appearance than honeysuckles, especially *Lonicera periclymenum*, the glorious woodbine of our hedges and woods, which bears such fragrant flowers. It is superb when allowed to trail over a rustic arch around a door, or an arch that straddles a path and separates one part of a garden from another. There are two superb forms of this climber:

L. p. 'Belgica' (early Dutch honeysuckle), with deep purple and red and yellow flowers during late spring and early summer.

L. p. 'Serotina' (late Dutch honeysuckle), with flowers that reveal red-purple shades on the outside and creamy-white on the inside from mid-summer to autumn.

'Mrs Cholmondeley': Single, pale blue, early summer to early autumn.

'Nellie Moser': Single, pale mauve-pink with crimson bar on each petal, early summer to late autumn.

'The President': Single, blue-purple flowers with paler stripes, early to late summer.

'Vyvyan Pennell': Single and double, violet-purple flowers flushed carmine, early summer and autumn.

In addition to these, several annual climbers are suitable for these purposes and are described on page 80.

A simple metal, wooden or even plastic arch like this one makes an eye-catching entrance to a different part of the garden. The addition of a couple of climbers makes it even more attractive.

Hedges for all gardens

Hedges are essential features in gardens. As well as being decorative, they create privacy, reduce the strength of wind and mark boundaries. They are also useful in separating different parts of the garden.

Easy-to-manage, fast-growing hedges are numerous and include fragrant and diminutive plants, such as lavender, as well as more vigorous and exceptionally large conifers. When planning which hedge to use, consider carefully what is appropriate. If you have close neighbours, an exceptionally fast-growing hybrid conifer such as × *Cupressocyparis leylandii* could be a disaster waiting to happen.

Flowering hedges

These have an informal and colourful nature and create a more restful ambience than neatly trimmed foliage hedges. Some of these flowering types are low and small enough to be used internally in a garden, or even on either side of a path. Their pruning is slightly more involved than just neatly clipping foliage types, but nothing to create a problem. Here are a few flowering hedges to consider, with indications of the level of pruning required.

Opposite: A hedge can be many things, all at the same time: a screen, a windbreak, an imposing entrance and a beautiful garden feature.

Getting the spacings right

When planting hedges it is necessary to space individual plants closer than when planted in a border. This ensures that a hedge with a thick and well-covered base is created quickly.

When planting hedges along a boundary, do not position plants directly on the perimeter line. Rather, plant them at least half the expected width of the hedge from the boundary. This prevents mature hedges from intruding on a neighbour's property.

Forsythia × *intermedia* **'Spectabilis' (golden bells):** Deciduous shrub with bright yellow flowers during spring.
Height: 1.8–2.1m (6–7ft)
Width: 60–75cm (2–2½ft)
Space plants: 38–45cm (15–18in)
Pruning: Clip established plants lightly, as soon as the flowers fade and the hedge loses its allure.

Fuchsia **'Riccartonii' (hardy fuchsia):** Deciduous shrub, best suited for mild and coastal areas, with beautiful red-and-purple flowers that flourish from mid-summer to autumn.
Height: 1–1.2m (3–4ft)
Width: 60–90cm (2–3ft)
Space plants: 30–38cm (12–15in)
Pruning: In spring, cut all stems to ground level.

Lavandula angustifolia **(lavender):** Hardy, evergreen shrub with pale, grey-blue flowers from mid- to late summer, and often into autumn.
Height: 75–90cm (2–3ft)
Width: 45–60cm (1½–2ft)
Space plants: 38–45cm (15–18in)
Pruning: Clip off dead flowers heads after flowering.

Potentilla fruticosa **(shrubby cinquefoil):** Hardy, deciduous shrub with buttercup-yellow flowers from late spring to late summer.
Height: 1.2–1.5m (4–5ft)
Width: 60cm (2ft)
Space plants: 25–30cm (10–12in)
Pruning: Clip off dead and dying flowers when they fade.

Roses as hedges

For devotees of roses in small gardens, planting a rose hedge is a further way to enhance the garden's beauty. There are many suitable roses.

'Ballerina': Single, blossom-pink flowers.
Height: 1.2m (4ft)
Space plants: 38–45cm (15–18in)
'Fru Dagmar Hastrup': Single, flesh-pink, delicate flowers.
Height: 1.2–1.5m (4–5ft)
Space plants: 60–75cm (2–2½ft)
'Roseraie de l'Haÿ': Double, rich wine-purple, scented flowers.
Height: 1.5m (5ft)
Space plants: 60–75cm (2–2½ft)
'White Pet': White, pompon-like flowers.
Height: 60cm (2ft)
Space plants: 30–38cm (12–15in)
'Windrush': Lemon-yellow, fragrant flowers.
Height: 1.2m (4ft)
Space plants: 45cm (1½ft)

Foliage hedges for small gardens

These are popular as they create screens throughout the year that help to protect gardens from cold winds. Here are a few of the less vigorous types:

***Buxus sempervirens* 'Suffruticosa' (dwarf box):** Evergreen, with small green leaves.
Height: 30–45cm (12–18in)
Width: 25–30cm (10–12in)
Space plants: 25–30cm (10–12in)
***Ligustrum ovalifolium* (privet):** Evergreen or semi-evergreen (depending on the climate) with glossy, mid-green leaves. Also, a yellow-leaved form, but less vigorous.
Height: 1.2–1.8m (4–6ft)
Width: 60–75cm (2–2½ft)
Space plants: 30–38cm (12–15in)
Lonicera nitida* (Chinese honeysuckle):** Evergreen with small green leaves. Also a golden-leaved form (L. n.* 'Baggeson's Gold'**).
Height: 90cm–1.5m (3–5ft)
Width: 45–60cm (1½–2ft)
Space plants: 30–38cm (12–15in)

Mixed foliage hedges

These are exceptionally attractive, but need careful planting and care to prevent a vigorous plant dominating its partner.
Yellow and green privet: Use a combination of *Ligustrum ovalifolium* (green-leaved) and *L. o.* 'Aureum' (yellow-leaved) privet. Position plants 30–38cm (12–15in) apart, using two of the yellow-leaved forms between each green type. After planting, cut back all shoots by a half or two-thirds to encourage bushiness at the hedge's base.
Variegated holly and green conifers: This is an unusual combination. Use a blend of two variegated hollies to one plant of *Chamaecyparis lawsoniana* (foliage has a parsley-like scent when bruised), and space plants 45cm (18in) apart. Do not prune them initially, although pruning will be needed at a later stage to create straight sides.

Brightening walls & fences

Even a small one-storey house has enough wall space for a few climbers, and invariably there are walls and fences throughout a garden that need brightening with flowers or attractive foliage.

Above: It is easy to personalize walls and fences with more than just plants. Bright paint, or decorative embellishments such as the pine cones that adorn the wooden fence above can make all the difference to an otherwise ordinary boundary.

Fast-growing annual and half-hardy annual climbers are described on pages 24 and 25, with other easily-manageable, suitable plants on page 27. Here, however, are some suggestions for other climbers which lend themselves particularly well to walls and fences, with ideas on specific ways to position them, sometimes in combination with other plants.

Summer displays

Abutilon vitifolium: A slightly tender, deciduous shrub that is best grown against a warm wall. From early to late summer it bears large, saucer-shaped, pale to deep blue flowers. It forms an attractive combination with the bright yellow, daisy-like flowers of *Senecio* 'Sunshine' and the sweetly-scented, yellow flowers of *Genista cinerea*, a broom that blooms during early and mid-summer.

***Ceanothus rigidus* (Californian lilac):** A half-hardy, evergreen shrub that welcomes the protection of a warm, sunny wall, where it bears long clusters of purple-blue flowers during spring and early summer. Plant yellow-flowered shrubs in front of it, such as shrubby potentillas which have a long flowering season.

***Cytisus battandieri* (Moroccan broom):** Deciduous or semi-evergreen shrub for planting against a warm, sunny wall. Pineapple-scented, golden-yellow flowers appear during mid-summer. They contrast well with the blue flowers of the herbaceous agapanthus.

***Lonicera japonica* 'Aureoreticulata':** Its green leaves have veins picked out in yellow. It is ideal on a small trellis with a sage and the variegated *Mentha rotundifolia* 'Variegata' (with creamy-white edges to the leaves) planted in front of it. Low stems of the lonicera will clamber through the sage and mint.

***Rosa ecae* 'Helen Knight'** (sometimes sold as **Rosa 'Helen Knight'**): This dainty, hardy, deciduous shrub rose with prickly stems and small, fern-like leaves displays yellow, saucer-shaped flowers during early summer. It forms an attractive duo with *Clematis montana* (mountain clematis).

***Solanum crispum* 'Glasnevin' (Chilean potato tree):** Scrambling, bushy climber with a semi-evergreen nature and pendulous clusters of purple-blue, star-shaped flowers with yellow anthers from early to late summer and often into autumn. It forms an ideal background for plants in containers, such as *Osteospermum* 'Prostratum' (previously known as *Dimorphotheca ecklonis* 'Prostrata') with its large, white flowers.

***Tropaeolum speciosum* (flame creeper):** A deciduous, perennial climber with long-stemmed, trumpet-shaped, scarlet flowers from mid-summer to autumn. It is often planted to scramble through shrubs, but can be used in combination with evergreen climbers such as the small-leaved and variegated ivy *Hedera helix* 'Goldheart'.

Winter displays

***Jasminum nudiflorum* (winter-flowering jasmine):** Hardy, deciduous, wall shrub with clusters of bright yellow, star-shaped flowers peppered along bare stems from early winter to early spring. It happily cohabits with the evergreen *Mahonia aquifolium*.

Spring displays

***Lonicera nitida* 'Baggesen's Gold' (yellow-leaved Chinese honeysuckle):** An evergreen shrub that can be trained to cloak a wall. Plant grape hyacinths (*Muscari*) underneath it to create a colour contrast in spring.

Below: Clematis, one of the most popular and ubiquitous of all plants, comes in many different varieties and lends itself well to growing up walls and fences and in containers.

Large-flowered clematis

These large-flowered hybrids drench gardens in colour from early to late summer, depending on the variety. They are superb for mixing and matching with other plants.

Clematis 'Ernest Markham', with velvety-red flowers mid-summer to autumn, colour contrasts with the variegated small-leaved ivy *Hedera helix* 'Goldheart'.

Clematis 'Jackmanii Superba', with dark violet-purple flowers from mid-summer to autumn, is ideal for planting as a colour contrast with the silvery-pink climbing rose 'New Dawn'.

Clematis 'Nelly Moser': Its pale mauve-pink flowers with crimson bars appear from early summer to late autumn. They are enhanced when *Zantedeschia aethiopica* 'Crowborough', with its rich, white arum-like flowers, is planted in front of it.

Scented roses for walls & fences

One way to enliven patios and courtyards, as well as boundary walls and fences, is to plant scented rambling roses and other climbers among them. Some can also be trained to cover pergolas. Here are a few unusual yet enlivening fragrances to consider.

Apple:

'François Juranville': Rambling rose, with glowing pink, double flowers with a tint of gold at their centres. Ideal for covering a large arch or pergola.

'Paul Transon': Rambling rose displaying coppery-orange to salmon flowers in small clusters. Plant it to cover a small pergola or arch.

Cloves:

'Blush Noisette': Climbing rose with semi-double, lilac-pink flowers. It grows well against a wall.

Fruity:

'Leander': Climber (English rose): Small, apricot-yellow, double, flowers in large clusters. Ideal for covering a wall.

Musk:

'Paul's Himalayan Musk': Rambling rose, with blush-pink flowers that reveal a rich, musk-like fragrance; borne in large, dainty clusters. Very vigorous rose, so train over a large pergola or plant it to climb into a tree.

Myrrh:

'Constance Spry': Climber (English rose) bearing exceptionally large, cup-shaped and paeony-like, clear rose-pink flowers. It is ideal for covering a wall.

'Cressida': Climber (English rose) with apricot-pink, full-petalled flowers. It is excellent when trained up a wall.

Orange:

'The Garland': Rambling rose with small, creamy-salmon flowers with quilted petals and a daisy-like appearance. It is ideal for planting to grow over a small arch or pergola.

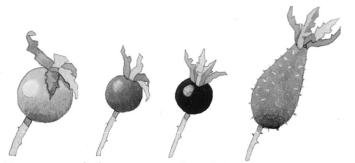

Roses with attractive hips

The fruits of roses are known as hips. Some are bottle-shaped, whereas others are elongated or prickly. Whatever their shape or colour, they offer a further way to liven up gardens.
From left to right: Large, red and round: *Rosa rugosa scabrosa*;
Small, red and round: *Rosa virginiana*; **Small, black and round:**
Rosa pimpinellifolia (also known as *R. spinosissima*);
Elongated: *Rosa moyessi* 'Geranium'.

Paeony:
'Gerbe Rose': Rambling rose with soft-pink flowers tinted cream. Plant it to cover an arch. Also ideal as a pillar rose.

Primrose:
'Adeläide' d'Orléans': Rambling rose with small, creamy-white, semi-double flowers. It is superb for trailing over arches and pergolas.

Sweet pea:
'Mme Grégoire Staechelin': Climbing rose with glowing coral-pink flowers flushed red. Vigorous and hardy, and ideal for a cold or exposed wall.

Sweetly fragrant climbers for walls

The range of scented climbers is wide, and they come in a rainbow of colours to suit all tastes and to contrast with any coloured background. For example, yellow- or red-flowered roses are highlighted by white walls, while red brick walls contrast with white, soft blue and lemon flowers.

Here are a few sweetly-scented climbers to choose for a scent-and-colour co-ordinated display:

'Étoile de Hollande, Climbing': Deep crimson and double.
'Guinée': Dark, velvety-scarlet, double flowers with black shading.
'Lawrence Johnston': Bright, clear yellow, large, semi-double flowers.
'Mme Alfred Carrière': White flowers slightly tinted fresh pink.
'Zéphirine Drouhin': Bright, carmine-pink, semi-double flowers. Grows well against cold walls.

The climbing Hybrid Tea rose 'Compassion' mixes well here with the shrub rose Rose 'Copenhagen', *antirrhinum* and *tanecetum*.

Other scented climbers

In addition to roses, many other climbers have flowers with unusual fragrances.

Cowslip-scented plants:
Clematis rehderiana: Deciduous, with greenish-yellow, bell-shaped flowers.

Hawthorn-scented plants:
Clematis flammula (fragrant virgin's bower): Deciduous, with white flowers borne in large, lax clusters.

Rich-smelling, honey-like plants:
Lonicera × italica (previously known as *L. × americana*): Semi-evergreen or deciduous, with white or cream flowers.
Lonicera × heckrottii: Deciduous and shrub-like, with yellow flowers flushed purple.

Jasmine-scented plants:
Jasminum officinale (common white jasmine): Deciduous, with white flowers.

Paths & steps

Garden paths and steps are too often ignored and neglected. Yet the addition of a few colourful plants along their edges or between their stones can swiftly transform them into important parts of the garden infrastructure that add to its overall effect.

Plants in natural stone paths

Paths formed of natural stone paving can be enlivened by planting low-growing plants in them. These plants introduce a further facet to paths, but need care and attention throughout the year. During spring and summer, take care not to step on the plants or run over them with a wheelbarrow. Also, in winter do not use salt to de-freeze frozen paving stones, nor use a shovel to remove snow from the path. However, minor problems such as these should not deter you from planting attractive plants in natural stone paths that will brighten and improve them in no time at all. Plants to consider include:

Unwanted grass and weeds growing between the cracks of a path can be the bane of a gardener's life. However, replace them with plants you do want to see, and the foliage- and flower-filled cracks become a positive feature.

Acaena microphylla **(New Zealand burr):** Grows about 5cm (2in) high and spreads to 45cm (18in). Crimson burrs from mid-summer onwards. Also, *A. buchananii*, 2.5–5cm (1–2in) high and spreading to 60cm (2ft), with amber-brown burrs.

Antennaria dioica **'Rosea' (cat's ears):** Mat-forming up to 45cm (18in) wide, with grey-green leaves and deep pink flowers during early summer.

Dianthus deltoides **(maiden pink):** Ideal for planting near the edges of paths, with flowers throughout much of summer; colours from white to pink and red.

Saxifraga burseriana: Forms a mat about 5cm (2in) high and spreading to 30cm (12in) of blue-grey leaves; pure-white flowers during late spring.

Thymus serpyllum **(wild thyme):** Mat-forming up to 7.5cm (3in) high and spreading to 45cm (18in). Grey-green leaves and flowers in a range of colours from early to late summer.

Brightening the edges of paths

The edges of paths are soon improved by planting flowering or foliage plants alongside them. They help to soften the often stark outlines of paths and to make them appear part of a garden rather than just a utilitarian feature. For each of the recommended plants that follow, the spacings between them, as well as the distances from the edge of the path, are indicated. This ensures that when plants are mature they cover the path's edge but do not intrude too far towards the centre. Plants to consider include:

Aethionema **'Warley Rose':** It delights in a dry, sunny position, where it reveals deep-pink flowers on plants 10–15cm (4–6in) high during late spring and early summer. Space plants 30–38cm (12–15in) apart, and 15–20cm (6–8in) from the path's edge.

Armeria maritima **(thrift):** Tufted plant, forming clumps 15–20cm (6–8in) high and 25–30cm (10–12in) wide. Pink flowers in star-like heads appear throughout summer; several forms, including white and rose-red. Space plants 25cm (10in) apart and 13cm (5in) from the path's edge.

Saxifraga umbrosa **(Pyrenean saxifrage):** Plant a ribbon of this 30cm (12in) high, shade-loving plant with masses of pink, star-shaped flowers in sprays during late spring and early summer. Space the plants 23–30cm (9–12in) apart and 15–20cm (6–8in) from the path's edge.

Enlivening the sides of steps

Plant creeping or arching plants at the sides of steps to add colour and vitality to them. As well as clothing the sides of steps, these plants can be used to make very wide steps appear narrower and less bleak. Where steps are large and formed of natural stone paving, a few plants such as those suggested on the opposite page will create further colour.

Woodland steps

Woodland-style log and bark chipping steps are an inexpensive and attractive alternative to those made of conventional stone or brick. They are not difficult to construct: dig the soil out to the levels of steps required; lay 15cm (6in) of clean, free-draining rubble on each step; secure the logs with wooden stakes; top up with bark.

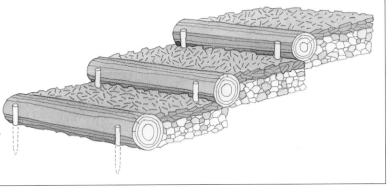

Brightening awkward corners

Few gardens do not have a difficult corner; perhaps cold and draughty, shaded for most of the day, or where the soil is cold and wet. Fortunately, many plants survive – even thrive – in these places. Here are a few quick and easy ways to brighten awkward corners.

Enlivening shady areas

The choice of shade-loving plants is wide; some will grow in the usually dry soil under trees, while others need more moisture.

Beneath trees

There is no substitute for brilliantly coloured flowers when it comes to brightening up an awkward corner. Some clematis will do surprisingly well in adverse conditions.

***Euphorbia amygdaloides robbiae*:** A ground-covering perennial, about 30cm (12in) high, with pale yellow-green bracts in clusters during early and mid-summer.

***Prunus laurocerasus* 'Otto Luyken' (cherry laurel):** Evergreen shrub, 1.2–1.5m (4–5ft) high and spreading to 1.8m (6ft); upright candles of white flowers during mid- and late summer.

***Ruscus aculeatus* (butcher's broom):** Evergreen shrub, about 75cm (2½ft) high and wide, with distinctive, spine-tipped leaves and sealing-wax red berries. Needs some moisture to thrive.

***Tellima grandiflora*:** Evergreen perennial, 45–60cm (1½–2ft) high and with a similar spread, with bright green, maple-like leaves and green-yellow, bell-shaped flowers during late spring and early summer.

Ground-covering plants for shade

***Ajuga reptans* (bugle):** Herbaceous perennial, about 25cm (10in) high and spreading to 45cm (1½ft), with whorls of blue flowers on upright shoots during early and mid-summer.

***Alchemilla mollis* (lady's mantle):** Herbaceous perennial, about 38cm (15in) high and wide, with light green, hairy leaves and clusters of yellow-green flowers throughout summer.

***Lamium galeobdolon* 'Florentinum'** (earlier known as ***L. g.* 'Variegatum'**): Perennial, 15–30cm (6–12in) high and spreading to about 45cm (1½ft), with silver-flushed evergreen leaves and spikes of yellow flowers during early and mid-summer.

Other plants for beneath trees

Hedera (ivies as ground-cover)
Helleborus
Mahonia
Vinca (periwinkle)

Ferns for shady and moist corners

Hardy ferns are superb for livening shaded areas. They are also ideal for planting in shaded places around garden ponds.

Asplenium scolopendrium (hart's-tongue): Evergreen, up to 60cm (2ft) high and spreading to 50cm (20in), with bright green, upright, tongue-like leaves. Several forms have fronds with cristate edges and tips.

Matteuccia struthiopteris (ostrich feather fern): In spring it develops a rosette of fronds that resemble a large shuttle-cock. It is large, up to 1.2m (4ft) high and 60–90cm (2–3ft) wide.

Surviving strong sunlight

Hot, unshaded corners test all plants, but those native to warm, sunny areas have the ability to flourish. They usually have white or hairy leaves, or are covered in oily glands that help insulate them from high temperatures. Here are two groups of plants that not only grow in hotspots, but thrive.

Border plants for hot, dry soils

Acanthus spinosus (bear's breeches): Large, deeply-cut and spiny leaves and tall spikes of purple and white flowers during mid- and late summer.

Achillea filipendulina (yarrow): Finely-cut leaves and large clusters of lemon-yellow flowers from mid-summer to autumn.

Crambe cordifolia (colewort): Cabbage-type leaves and large sprays of white flowers during early summer.

Gypsophila paniculata (baby's breath): Grass-like leaves and loose clusters of white flowers throughout summer.

Nepeta × faassenii (catmint): Grey leaves and mauve-blue flowers throughout summer and into autumn.

Shrubs for dry, hot corners

Choisya ternata (Mexican orange blossom): Aromatic, glossy-green leaves and clusters of white flowers during late spring and early summer.

Cistus (rock roses): Many species, usually with large flowers during early and mid-summer.

Cytisus (broom): Many species; mainly yellow flowers.

Genista (broom): Many species; mainly with yellow flowers.

Rosmarinus officinalis (rosemary): Aromatic foliage, with spikes of small, mauve flowers during early summer.

If the soil or climate in your awkward corner is so bad that few plants are happy, consider laying a simple mosaic design like the one above, made up from bits of old ceramic tiles and pots.

Other ground-covering plants for shade

Bergenia (elephant's ears)
Epimedium (barrenwort)
Euonymus fortunei 'Emerald 'n' Gold'
Pachysandra terminalis 'Variegata'

Surviving buffeting winds

Many gardens are buffeted by wind, even in the mildest areas. Wind swirls between buildings, while eddies develop close to walls. For large and exposed areas, hedges can help, but for those small and awkward corners found in most gardens, it is the plants themselves that must be resilient.

Above: Plants in awkward corners can be afforded protection by hedges, screens, furniture and features, but if these are not available, choose hardy types that can manage on their own.

Coastal areas suffer from the further hazard of sea-salt spray, which can burn, distort and kill plants – but there are widely-available plants that will tolerate even these conditions.

Shrubs for windy, coastal areas

Although ideal for seaside sites, these shrubs also thrive in other windswept areas where it is difficult to establish and cultivate plants.

***Elaeagnus pungens* 'Maculata':** Hardy, slow-growing, evergreen shrub, about 2.4m (8ft) high and wide, with oval, leathery, glossy-green leaves splashed with gold. It is ideal for creating a colour contrast with the purple-leaved *Cotinus coggygria* 'Royal Purple'.

***Hippophae rhamnoides* (sea buckthorn):** Very hardy, deciduous and bushy shrub, 1.8–2.4m (6–8ft) high and wide, with narrow, silvery leaves. Bright orange berries appear from autumn to late winter. Birds do not usually eat these berries and therefore it creates an attractive feature in winter.

Olearia macrodonta (daisy bush):
Evergreen and 1.8–2.1m (6–7ft) high and wide, it bears holly-like, mid-green leaves and small, daisy-like flowers in tight clusters during mid-summer. It survives wind and salt spray, but is slightly tender in very cold areas.

Symphoricarpos albus (snowberry): Hardy, deciduous and suckering shrub, 1.5–1.8m (5–6ft) high and spreading to 2.1m (7ft) – it forms a thicket. It is mainly grown for its white berries, which persist from autumn to late winter. It is ideal for a windswept bed between houses or walls.

Other shrubs for coastal areas

Elaeagnus × *ebbingei*: Evergreen, with leathery, silvery-grey leaves.

Euonymus japonicus **(spindle tree):** Bushy and evergreen, with glossy, green leaves. Several variegated forms.

Olearia × *haastii* **(daisy bush):** Hardy and evergreen, with white, daisy-like flowers during mid-summer.

Pittosporum tenuifolium: Slightly tender evergreen shrub with wavy-edged leaves.

Spartium junceum **(Spanish broom):** Hardy and deciduous, with rush-like green stems and yellow, pea-like flowers during early and mid-summer. It is very fast growing.

Tamarix tetrandra **(tamarisk):** Hardy and deciduous, with wispy foliage and bright pink flowers during late spring. It survives very windy areas wonderfully well.

Border plants for windswept corners

Many herbaceous plants survive strong winds once they are established and growing strongly. Here are a few of them:

Chelone obliqua **(turtlehead):** Grows 45–60cm (1½–2ft) high, with upright stems bearing terminal clusters of deep rose, snapdragon-like flowers during mid- and late summer. Space plants 30–45cm (1–1½ft) apart. It forms an attractive colour-contrasting partnership with

Leucanthemum × *superbum* (the Shasta daisy, and still better known as *Chrysanthemum maximum*).

Heuchera sanguinea **(coral flower):** Grows 30–45cm (1–1½ft) high, with masses of slender stems that bear bright red, bell-shaped flowers throughout summer. Space plants 38cm (15in) apart.

Liatris spicata **(blazing star):** Grows about 60cm (2ft) high and reveals upright, wand-like spires of pink-purple flowers during late summer. Space plants 38cm (15in) apart. It harmonizes with many plants, including kniphofias (red hot pokers) and *Bergenia* 'Silberlicht'.

Platycodon grandiflorus **(balloon flower):** Grows 30–60cm (1–2ft) high and produces balloon-shaped buds that open throughout summer to reveal light blue, saucer-shaped flowers. Space plants 38cm (15in) apart.

This screen hedge of ***Rosmarinus officinalis*** **is bolstered by an attractively shaped picket fence and will thrive in hot, windy conditions.**

Other border plants for windswept corners

Anaphalis triplinervis (pearly everlasting)
Asters (short types)
Coreopsis grandiflora
Geranium endressii
Persicaria affinis (but previously known as *Polygonum affine*)
Potentilla atrosanguinea
Sedum spectabile (ice plant)
Stokesia laevis (Stokes' aster)
Veronica spicata

Container Gardening

One of the quickest and most effective ways of transforming the look and ambience of any garden is to decorate it with richly-planted containers. Brightly-coloured flowers and leaves make everybody feel good, and in containers they can be positioned close to a house, making them immediately noticeable.

The great advantage of containers is that they can be positioned wherever they will have the most dramatic impact. More often than not they are positioned on patios, near entrances or beneath windows – the places in the garden where they are most likely to be seen.

Garden containers come in all shapes and sizes and range dramatically in price, whether they be hanging-baskets, windowboxes, troughs, standard pots or dramatic amphorae. Whichever you use, they will transform your garden and enhance the backdrop of your house.

Positioning containers in attractive combinations, perhaps at the sides of doors and windows, alongside patios or to decorate long, bland walls, is a yearly opportunity to create different shape and colour features. Here are a few short-cut arrangements to consider.

Hanging-baskets:
● Position a hanging-basket either side of a front door. Ensure that each basket is suspended about twice its width from the door's edge to allow for the display's width when the plants are mature.
● Secure hanging-baskets either side of a window; ensure that the foliage slightly cuts across the window's vertical edges. Position a large trough or planter under the window.
● Use hanging-baskets in a combination with a windowbox. To prevent the heads or shoulders of passers-by knocking hanging-baskets, position tubs underneath; but not where water from the basket drips on them.
● Suspend hanging-baskets from the edges of verandahs, summer-houses and car-ports, to brighten up these structures.

● Use hanging-baskets to clothe walls, but not near corners.

Wall-baskets and troughs:

● Use wall-baskets on walls, between windows and to clothe bland walls.
● Use wall-baskets in combination with two upright, slow-growing conifers in large pots or tubs positioned on either side.
● Place troughs on low walls at the edges of patios. Alternatively, create a false wall by positioning troughs on bricks.
● Position troughs at the edges of flat roofs. Place each container on 2.5cm-square pieces of wood to enable water to drain from the compost. It also allows the trough to be picked up easily.

Pots and other containers:

A group of pots in various sizes and shapes in a corner of a patio creates colour over a long period. It also becomes a focal point, perhaps deflecting attention from a less attractive part of a garden.
● Position urns at the tops of steps. Placed on plinths, urns will create an even more striking and distinguished effect.
● Wooden tubs, planted with daffodils and polyanthus, look good on either

side of an otherwise bare entrance.
● Two large, white tubs planted with half-standard sweet bay trees look superb on either side of an entrance.
● Square, wooden, Versailles-type planters are ideal for *agapanthus* (African lily), especially when positioned along the edge of a patio.

Garden containers are available in many shapes, sizes and colours and can be used to accommodate anything from annuals to small fruit trees. They are certainly one of the most versatile of all garden features.

Pots & tubs for all places

These are oases for plants of all kinds, from foliage and flowering border plants to bulbs, shrubs and trees, as well as conifers. There are many plants to choose from; here are some of the more easily-grown ones.

Border plants for pots and tubs

Attractive leaves:

Acorus gramineus 'Ogon': Narrow, arching leaves with golden variegations.

Aegopodium podagraria 'Variegatum' (variegated ground elder): Green leaves edged and splashed in ivory.

Carex oshimensis 'Evergold' (previously known as *C. morrowii* 'Evergold'): Arching leaves, variegated green and yellow.

Festuca glauca 'blauglut' (previously known as *F. g.* 'Blue Glow', and popularly as sheep's fescue): Hummocks of blue-green, narrow leaves.

Hakonechloa macra 'Alboaurea': Graceful, narrow leaves vividly variegated gold and buff, with touches of bronze.

Hebe × andersonii 'Variegata' (variegated shrubby veronica): Shrubby, with mid-green leaves variegated cream.

Hosta sieboldiana (plantain lily): Large, oval, glossy, mid-green leaves and dull white flowers tinged purple.

Opposite: This superb Argyranthemum frutescens *(marguerite), grown in an ornate terracotta pot, imbues its surroundings with stately elegance.*

Phormium tenax (New Zealand flax): Masses of long, strap-like leaves; some varieties are variegated, others just one colour.

Stachys byzantina (lamb's tongue): Oval, soft, white-silvery leaves.

Attractive flowers:

Agapanthus campanulatus (African lily): Herbaceous, with strap-like leaves and umbrella-like heads of pale blue flowers during late summer.

Anthemis punctata cupaniana: Cushion-forming, with bright, white, daisy-like flowers during early and mid-summer.

Bergenia cordifolia (elephant's ears): Large, rounded, leathery leaves and clustered heads of bell-shaped, lilac-rose flowers during early and mid-spring.

Dicentra spectabilis (bleeding heart): Grey-green leaves and rosy-red, locket-shaped flowers during late spring and early summer. There is also a white-flowered form.

Helleborus orientalis (lenten rose): Dark green evergreen leaves and saucer-shaped cream flowers flecked with crimson during late winter and into spring.

Sedum spectabile: Grey-green leaves and large, clustered heads bearing pink flowers during late summer and autumn.

Beautiful bulbs for tubs and pots

Many bulbs create bright displays in spring: plant spring-flowering bulbs in late summer or early autumn.

Colourful hostas for pots and tubs

Hosta 'Blue Moon': Small, deep-blue leaves and greyish-mauve flowers.

Hosta 'Gold Standard': Gold leaves delicately edged dark green.

Hosta 'Shade Fanfare': Green leaves with broad cream edges.

Hosta 'Wide Brim': Oval, blue-green leaves irregularly edged in cream to golden-yellow.

Hosta 'Zounds': Large, deeply-puckered, yellow leaves.

Hyacinthus (**hyacinths**): Upright and soldier-like, with heads tightly clustered with blue, white, pink or red flowers during late spring. Plant 13–15cm (5–6in) deep and 5–7.5cm (2–3in) apart.

Muscari armeniacum (**grape hyacinth**): Clustered heads of deep blue flowers. Plant bulbs 6cm (2in) deep and slightly apart.

Narcissus (**trumpet daffodils**): Ideal for tubs, pots and troughs, preferably on their own. Plant bulbs with their tops about 7.5cm (3in) deep, and slightly apart.

Tulipa (**tulips**): Select short, single early varieties and plant with their noses 10cm (4in) deep, and 5cm (2in) apart from one another.

Lilies for summer colour

Lilies have a distinguished appearance and several are ideal for growing in tubs and large pots, where they create dramatic displays in summer. The following lilies have the bonus of scent. Plant lilies in autumn.

Lilium auratum (golden-rayed lily of Japan): Bowl-shaped, brilliant-white flowers with golden bands in late summer.

Lilium candidum (Madonna lily): Bell-shaped, pure-white flowers with golden anthers in early and mid-summer.

Lilium hansonii: Turk's-cap, pale orange-yellow flowers with brown spots in early and mid-summer.

Lilium longiflorum (Easter lily): Trumpet-shaped, white flowers with golden pollen in mid- and late summer.

Lilium speciosum: Bowl-shaped, white flowers shaded crimson in late summer.

Glorious hanging-baskets

Hanging-baskets create spectacular displays throughout the summer. They are formed of flowering and attractively-foliaged plants, in colour mixtures or as single-colour themes, and will brighten drab doorways, windows and walls.

A good example of how effectively a multi-coloured hanging-basket display can brighten an otherwise drab brick wall.

Each year, seed companies introduce new varieties of flowers for planting in hanging-baskets. These plants vary in size, shape and colour, but all have several important qualities:
● They must be able to flourish in small amounts of compost and, preferably, not be exceptionally invasive of their neighbours.

● Preferably, those that flower should be in bloom when planted in late spring or early summer.
● They must respond well to regular feeding, from mid- to late summer, which encourages the continuing development of flowers.
● Plants must not be susceptible to pests and diseases. For example, although trailing nasturtiums are attractive, they invariably attract black-fly.

Clues to selecting plants

Single-colour hanging-baskets create dominant displays, but ensure they harmonize with their background.

In mixed baskets, combine foliage plants with flowers. Many foliage plants are better able to survive adverse weather than flowering types.

Three mix-and-match recipes

1) Dwarf marigolds, cascading petunias and trailing lobelia. As an alternative to petunias, use busy Lizzies.
2) Trailing lobelia to cloak the sides, *Helichrysum petiolare* 'Limelight' to create width and colour, and ivy-leaved geraniums to provide both colour and leaf-shape contrast.
3) Cascading fuchsias create an informal outline that harmonizes well with trailing lobelia and nasturtiums.

Keeping plants healthy

To keep hanging-baskets attractive, plants require daily attention throughout summer.
- If baskets are put outdoors too early, and a light frost is forecast, place several layers of newspaper over the plants.
- Water the compost every day – sometimes twice – during hot weather.
- Feed plants every ten to fourteen days when they are established and growing strongly. Add fertilizer to the water when watering plants, but first ensure that the compost is moist.
- Pinch off dead or faded flowers as they appear, to encourage the development of further blooms.

Stark, boring windows and walls can be speedily enhanced by the addition of one or two baskets.

This balcony has been immediately transformed by the three mixed baskets suspended above it.

Planting a hanging-basket

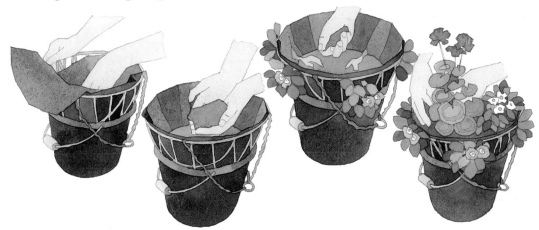

1 Place a wire-framed hanging-basket in the top of a bucket to hold it firm while being planted. Line the basket with black polythene and mould it to the basket's shape; cut it off 5–7.5cm (2–3in) above the rim. Later, it will need re-trimming.

2 Place a handful of moist peat in the base, then add and firm a proprietary hanging-basket compost to about half the basket's depth. Make 5cm (2in) long slits in the plastic, about 10cm (4in) apart and level with the surface of the compost.

3 Push the roots of trailing plants through the slits, spread them and lightly cover with compost. Then, plants can be placed in the basket's top. Put a dominant, cascading plant in the centre; check that the top of its soil-ball is 12–18mm (½–¾in) below the rim.

4 Position further trailing plants around the central plant, again with their tops below the rim. Cover and firm compost around the soil-balls, so that the surface is 12mm (½in) below the rim. Cut the plastic level with the rim and thoroughly water the compost.

5 Form a thin layer of sphagnum moss over the surface; this creates an attractive foil for the plants and helps to prevent compost being washed over the sides when the basket is watered. Again water the compost. If the risk of frost has passed, suspend the basket outside.

Glorious windowboxes

Windowboxes are the two-way mirrors of the gardening world; they can be admired from both outside and inside a house. And the fragrance of some plants is a rich bonus. Unlike hanging-baskets, which have only a summer season, windowboxes can be rich in colour throughout the year.

Seasonal philosophy

Windowboxes are entire gardens in microcosm, and considerably easier and quicker to manage than the real thing. The greatest advantage windowboxes have to offer is that they can be easily planted up to provide genuine year-round colour. With just a little time and effort and some careful planning, you can create beautiful, fragrant displays for all seasons that can be fully appreciated by admirers from both inside and outside the house.

It is necessary to plan your displays carefully and to have three separate inner boxes available that can be placed inside an attractive outer windowbox when their respective flowering seasons arrive.

Spring-flowering windowboxes: These are mainly formed of bulbous plants, such as daffodils, hyacinths and tulips. Additionally, they are interplanted with biennials, such as wallflowers. These boxes should be planted in late summer or early autumn,

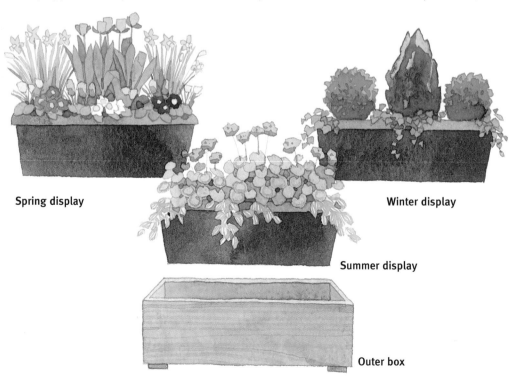

Spring display

Winter display

Summer display

Plant an inner windowbox for every season, and it is easy to ensure year-round colour on the window-sills of your home.

Outer box

placed in a sheltered position outdoors and put in an outer windowbox in early spring when their plants are starting to burst into flower. During winter, keep the compost moderately moist, but not waterlogged.

Summer-flowering windowboxes: Mainly formed of summer-flowering, half-hardy annuals and planted in late spring or early summer, these windowboxes create spectacular displays until the frosts of autumn. As soon as the spring-flowering display is over, replace it with the summer one.

Winter displays: These are formed of dwarf conifers, evergreen shrubs when young and small, and low, winter-flowering shrubs such as *Erica carnea*. There are also varieties of this heath that have colourful foliage, such as *E. c.* 'Foxhollow' (bright gold).

Planting or plunging?

There are two ways to fill windowboxes with plants.

Planting in compost: Normally used for spring-flowering displays, when bulbs and biennials are planted. It can also be employed for summer displays. Place broken pieces of clay pots (crocks) over drainage holes in an inner box, then a 12mm (½in) layer of gravel chippings. Over this, place and firm compost and plant directly into it.

Plunging pots: These are ideal for winter displays, where some plants are left in position for several years but then need to be individually changed. Summer displays can be given the same treatment, where failing plants need to be changed to pep up the display.

Drainage holes in the base of the inner box are covered with crocks, then a layer of peat. Plants are stood on top, with moist peat packed around them. The peat helps to keep plants cool in summer and reduces the need to apply water to plants. As an alternative to peat, pea-shingle can be used and is ideal for winter displays.

Double flower power

Extra colour is easily created by positioning one windowbox above another. Leave about 45cm (1½ft) between them, with the lower box supported on brackets secured to a wall. Colour-harmonizing the boxes creates further interest. For example, if a windowbox is positioned against a white wall, paint it yellow, if placed against a red-brick wall then paint it blue, and so on. Anything goes with versatile windowboxes.

Windowboxes will work with any type of window – it is just a case of positioning the box appropriately. From left to right, above: sash window; casement window; outward-opening plastic-framed windows.

Sash or casement windows

The type of window influences the position of a windowbox.

Sash windows: These are windows that open upwards and therefore do not disturb plants in windowboxes positioned directly on ledges. This type of window also enables the scent from fragrant plants to waft indoors.

Casement windows: These are windows that are hinged at their sides and therefore, when opened, sweep out and over the ledge. For this type of window, secure windowboxes 20–25cm (8–10in) below the ledge. Ensure brackets supporting the windowbox are firm.

Plastic-framed windows: Some are designed like casement windows, while others hinge in a cantilever action and open out in a wide arc over the ledge. Whatever the type, it usually means that the windowbox has to be supported on brackets below the ledge.

Wall-baskets & mangers

Wall-baskets and mangers are increasingly popular as they offer the opportunity to create large and dramatic displays of flowers and decorative foliage against walls. These create spectacular colour in spring and summer, usually at waist height.

Displaying wall-baskets and mangers

Because they are independent of soil at ground level, wall-baskets and mangers can be positioned wherever drives, paths or pavements abut walls. Another intrinsic advantage of these planting vessels is that because they are not at ground level, rubbish does not collect around them.

Where flowerbeds are positioned beneath wall-baskets and mangers, colour harmonies or contrasts can easily be created between the two features.

Combine wall-baskets and mangers with plants in tubs or large pots. For example, after planting these features, position a tall plant on either side, such as half-standard fuchsias or tall, columnar conifers.

Small wall-baskets are ideal for positioning on walls either side of a front door. They may also be used on balcony walls, where they are less susceptible than hanging-baskets to damage from strong, blustery winds.

When using a wall-basket or manger on a wall between two windowboxes, position it slightly lower than the boxes. If placed at the same level, it creates a ribbon of colour that bisects the house. Positioning a manger or wall-basket slightly lower creates a better design and does not confuse the eye.

Simple but sure displays

Some seed-raised plants have been developed to survive rain and storms – and even hot weather. The following plants will repay careful cultivation with fine displays whatever the conditions:

Camissonia cheiranthifolia: Bright, canary-yellow flowers over a long period.

Impatiens **'Bruno':** A busy Lizzie with large flowers in mixed colours.

Impatiens **'Mega Orange Star':** A busy Lizzie with large orange flowers with white bars.

Petunia **'Prism Sunshine':** Large, bright yellow flowers that fade cream; veined in lime green.

Petunia **'Storm Mixed':** Colour mixture – white, pink, salmon and lavender.

Spraguea umbellata **'Powder Puffs':** Known as 'pussy paws', these plants produce fur-like, powder-pink flowers, at least on those that survive moderate droughts.

Planting considerations

Winter displays in wall-baskets and mangers are not usually possible, as bulbs and biennials, such as wallflowers, are planted directly into the compost in late summer or autumn in preparation for a spring display. As soon as spring displays fade, summer displays are planted directly into new or revitalized compost.

The use of containers on walls need not be confined to proprietary brands and standard shapes and sizes. The approach should be: 'if it will take a plant and it is attractive, why not hang it on the wall?' This way of thinking will also save you time and money....

Sizes and materials

There are mangers and wall-baskets to suit all walls.

Mangers are available in sizes from 30cm (12in) wide to about 70cm (28in), in about 10cm (4in) stages.

Wire-framed wall-baskets range in width from 23cm (9in) to 50cm (20in) wide.

Plastic and terracotta types are available in widths from 15cm (6in) to 25cm (10in)and come in a variety of different colours.

Planting a wall-basket or manger

Secure the basket or manger to a wall and line it with thick, black plastic, ensuring that it overlaps the back and front edges.

The plastic prevents compost falling out, conserves moisture in the compost and reduces the chance of excess water running down a wall.

Spread a 5cm (2in) layer of moist peat in the base, then add and firm equal parts peat-based compost and loam-based compost to within 2.5cm (1in) of the rim.

Use a sharply-pointed knife to puncture the plastic along the base of the basket's front to encourage water to escape and not to run down the wall.

Troughs for all places

Troughs are versatile and can be used in many ways on patios, terraces and balconies. They can also be secured to bland walls to create colour. Here are a few ways to use them for instant, short-cut effects.

Above: This large purpose-built stone trough has been constructed alongside an otherwise unremarkable wall and filled with a variety of richly-planted containers.

- Position troughs at the edges of flat roofs. Use a combination of 15–20cm (6–8in) high plants and trailing types. Avoid tall plants, as these will be buffeted and damaged by strong wind.
- Place troughs on low walls. Use loam-based compost to create a firmer base than peat types and, again, use a combination of low and trailing plants.
- Position troughs at the edges of patios to create a low, false wall. Taller plants can be used with these ground-based troughs than when positioned on walls.
- Place troughs at the sides of balconies; use plants up to 38cm (15in) high, together with trailing plants that can cascade through the railings and soften the often harsh outline of a balcony's base.
- Secure troughs to the sides of walls; use the same type of supporting brackets used to support windowboxes. Upright and cascading plants can be used.
- Position troughs at the edges of formal ponds to soften their often clinical outlines. Use low and trailing plants.
- Raising rustic, wooden troughs on 20cm (8in) high legs makes them more imposing and attractive.

Plants for troughs

The main types of plants used in troughs are those also planted in windowboxes, especially if the trough is raised and plants

Brighten a balcony with one or more troughs across its full width.

Stand a trough atop a wall and you create an instant vertical feature.

An ornate trough upon a plinth will impart an air of grandeur.

are able to cascade freely. Troughs on the ground, or raised only 5cm (2in), are best planted with upright and bushy plants.

Colour and shape combinations:

Summer display – For a flower and foliage medley use trailing ivy-leaved pelargoniums along the front and sides, interspersed with sweet alyssum. At the ends and in the middle, position small variegated sages, such as *Salvia officinalis* 'Tricolor', with the main colour provided by the seed-raised Dahlia 'Redskin', which displays bright flowers and deep bronze-green leaves.

Winter display – This medley of evergreen and flowering plants creates colour throughout winter. Plant a young *Juniperus horizontalis* 'Bar Harbour' at one end, with the mound-like *Hebe pinguifolia* 'Pagei' at the other. Between them, plant a small rosemary and *Erica carnea* 'Springwood White'.

Culinary herbs

Troughs on patios provide ideal homes for many culinary herbs, especially relatively low-growing types. Herbs to use include:
Chives have green, tubular leaves and star-shaped blue flowers.
Thyme has a trailing nature and is ideal for positioning at the edges of troughs. For added colour, try the golden-leaved thyme.
Parsley, raised annually from seeds, is best left in its pot and just placed in the trough.
Mint has invasive roots and is another herb best left in a pot and placed in a trough.
Balm has a refreshing bouquet to its leaves. Use the golden balm for extra colour.

Materials for troughs

Troughs are made from a wide variety of materials and include:
Wooden troughs: these have a rustic nature and keep plants cool in summer. They are especially attractive when mounted on legs.
Reconstituted stone troughs: these are heavy and expensive, but very durable and attractive.
Fibreglass troughs: durable and light and particularly useful on roofs and balconies. Both modern styles and reproductions of traditional designs are available.
Plastic troughs: these have a limited life and some are degraded by strong sunlight. However, they are inexpensive and make ideal homes for plants for a season or two.
Terracotta troughs: relatively heavy, with a 'natural' appearance and the ability to harmonize well with most plants.

This tree-stump has been imaginatively converted into an attractive spring container brimming with primula. With a little hollowing-out and the addition of a suitable growing medium, it has ceased to be an eyesore.

Unusual containers

Creating unusual and distinctive containers for plants helps to personalize a garden. You might choose to convert an old wheelbarrow or paint and plant up some old car tyres – different effects are simple to create and need not take long to establish. Here are a few to consider.

A pensioned-off wheelbarrow, made of either wood or metal, can be turned into a novel container for summer-flowering plants. Check the wheelbarrow's structure before you begin and reinforce weak joints with brackets. Drill drainage holes in the base so that the barrow will drain freely. Place the wheelbarrow in position and add a layer of coarse drainage material to the base. Fill to within 36mm (1¼in) of the rim with well-drained compost. Plant summer-flowering bedding plants, such as half-hardy annuals, as soon as all risk of frost has passed.

Old tyres can also be used to create unusual containers in the garden. Stack and secure three or four tyres together with wire. Select a plastic bucket with a top about the width of the hole at the centre of the tyres. Pierce holes in its base and position it inside the hole; place bricks underneath its base to make the top of the bucket level with the top of the tyres. Add

Recycling old growing-bags

Growing-bags used the previous year for tomatoes or lettuces can be used during the following year for summer-flowering bedding plants. In spring, mix a general fertilizer with the compost in a bag and plant half-hardy bedding plants as soon as all risk of frost has passed.

Old growing-bags make inexpensive containers for placing at the edge of a balcony or flat roof; use plenty of trailing plants, so that they become swamped with colour.

coarse drainage material to the bucket, then compost. Both spring- and summer-flowering displays can be created in very little time at all. Paint the tyres white for a more aesthetic effect.

Old metal watering-cans, painted white or yellow, can be most attractive when filled with summer-flowering bedding plants. Use trailing plants, such as lobelias, to clothe the sides.

Redundant Victorian chimney pots, ideally about 90cm in height, can be easily secured upright on well-drained soil; fill their bases with coarse drainage material and top up with well-drained compost. Plant them with summer-flowering trailing plants that will drench their sides in colour. The addition of a cascading fuchsia will bring further authority to the display.

A small wine cask, about 60cm (2ft) in height, can make an especially attractive plant container when a window is cut out of its side and the cask is then supported either on several bricks or a cradle formed of short rustic poles. Drill drainage holes in the side of the cask opposite the window. Plant it with cascading and trailing summer-flowering bedding plants, once again aiming to produce as colourful an effect as possible.

Sink gardens

Old stone sinks planted with small rock garden plants, alpines, miniature bulbs and conifers create distinctive displays and are usually at their best in spring.

Preparing and planting

Thoroughly scrub the sink. Place it on four strong bricks, with a slight slope to the drainage hole.

Place a piece of crumpled wire-netting over the drainage hole.

Form a layer of broken clay pots in the base, then 2.5cm (1in) of pea-shingle and 2.5–4cm (1–1¾in) of moist peat.

Fill to within 2.5cm (1in) of the rim with a mixture of soil-based potting compost with extra peat and sharp sand.

After planting, add a 12mm (½in) thick layer of pea-shingle, with its surface 12mm (½in) below the rim.

Plants to choose
Small rock garden plants and alpines:
Androsace sarmentosa ‘Chumbyi’
Antennaria microphylla
Campanula cochleariifolia
Edraianthus pumilio
Erinus alpinus
Hebe buchananii ‘Minor’
Lewisia cotyledon

Small spring-flowering bulbs:
Iris danfordiae
Iris reticulata
Galanthus nivalis
Narcissus cyclamineus
Miniature conifers:
Chamaecyparis obtusa ‘Pygmaea’
Chamaecyparis pisifera ‘Nana’
Juniperus communis ‘Compressa’

An old wheelbarrow can look surprisingly attractive when imaginatively planted up, especially if it is made of wood, like this one.

Old stone sinks make ideal homes for miniature rock garden plants, as well as dwarf conifers and diminutive bulbs.

Decorative Garden Features

In addition to colourful plants, nothing brightens and enhances a garden more than a carefully planned range of garden features. Nowadays there is a huge variety of decorative features to choose from – whether you fancy a classical statue, an ornamental garden pond or a simple rustic pergola. The most important thing about decorative features is that they act simultaneously both as garden ornaments and as integral parts of the garden framework – a quality which often lends them a significance way beyond the expense or amount of effort required to create them in the first place. In a nutshell, a distinctive, decorative feature enhances the entire garden.

This chapter explores a large number of decorative features, ranging from miniature water gardens and ornate fences to romantic arbours and raised beds. They are all quick and easy to create.

Many of the features covered in this chapter are beautiful and eye-catching in their own right, but some require the addition of plants to make them really distinctive. Fences and gates, for example, can be replaced or modified to improve a garden no end, but they remain chiefly functional and are much enhanced by carefully selected plants positioned on or near them. There are numerous ideas and proposals for suitable planting schemes throughout the book, but refer to Chapter 3 in particular when deciding how to decorate any of the features described in the following pages.

Whichever decorative features you decide to incorporate in your garden, make sure they are suited to the overall size and style of what you already have. Without careful forethought you could end up with a too-dominant structure that detracts from other elements in the garden. Think hard about what your garden would really benefit from before you start buying or building...

This spectacular natural arch has actually been formed out of the branches of the sweeping tree growing behind it.

Glorious water

There is a magical quality to water that makes it the perfect medium for pleasing garden features; the sparkle and sound of water cascading over pebbles or spurting from a fountain has a soothing, restful effect that will add a welcome extra dimension to any garden.

Many water features, such as garden ponds, are time-consuming and expensive to construct, but there are a few that can be quickly and easily installed and that will transform your garden in no time at all. The other great advantage of the decorative water features that follow is that because they do not rely on expansive or deep areas of water, they are much safer for families with young children or pets. They also require far less maintenance and general upkeep than larger, more ambitious water features.

Patio water gardens

Patio water gardens are quick and easy to build and can be constructed out of relatively inexpensive and widely available materials. They have been used for centuries to brighten awkward corners or to relieve the monotony of large, paved areas; water gardens were an integral part of medieval Spanish patios.

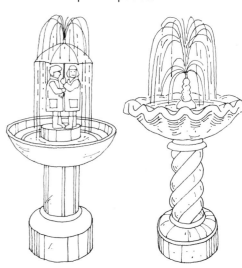

Fountain designs have for centuries incorporated people, animals and fish. This simple yet charming design features a couple sheltering from the 'rain' of the fountain.

This more ornate design echoes the mighty fountains of 18th-century classical French gardens and, set in an appropriate context, would impart easy style and elegance.

Lighting water features and patios

A few lights enhance patios no end and make them more usable, especially during spring and early autumn when daylight is short. The general area can be highlighted and plants given a fresh, radiant face. Pebble water gardens, statues and fountains also benefit from lights.

Spot lights: These can either be secured to walls or mounted on spikes driven into the ground, where they can be angled to create a range of lighting effects across the entire garden.

General lights: There are several types available, all intended to illuminate large areas; some come in the form of bollards, while others are mounted on posts.

Underwater lighting: In a pond, either alongside a patio or in a garden, submersible lights (some coloured) create exciting features. There are also lights that can be combined with fountains,

(Safety: Commission a good electrician to install and maintain the lights, especially those used in ponds.)

Generally miniature by definition, patio water gardens are ideal for fitting into corners, installing against walls or for use as 'stand-alone' features in the centre of a patio. As they need not be stocked with fish or plants, they are easy to maintain and to keep clean.

There are a variety of different patio water gardens to choose from:

Pebble ponds: The principle here is that water from a fountain splashes down over a pebble base, creating a rhythmic but irregular sound pattern while the sparkle of water splashing on an uneven surface creates attractive light patterns that will reflect across the garden on a summer's day (see illustrations page 77).

The fountain can be created by an upright column of water, or by water gushing out of a cherub's or animal's mouth secured to an ornamental wall. Decorative fountain 'mouths' are now widely available in most garden centres and DIY stores.

One simple and effective variation on the basic fountain is to position three square-shaped columns at different heights, from which water will tumble and cascade in varying degrees, creating more varied and pleasing visual and aural effects. The water will fall down onto the pebbles to be recycled by a small pump.

Another version of the pebble pond involves water spouting out of an ornamental water-pump and falling into a large, wide, basin of pebbles.

Fountain features

One of the most attractive and effective of water features is the stand-alone fountain. There are many different types, but typically such a fountain is formed of an ornate pedestal or a statue holding a pot or urn from which water flows. Stand-alone fountains are ideal for brightening up patios and other level, paved areas.

These unusual 'pod' fountains bring an other-worldly quality to their surroundings.

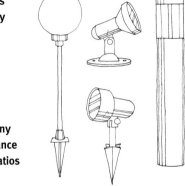

Garden lighting comes in many different forms and will enhance a water feature, as well as patios and courtyards.

Selecting a fountain

When choosing a fountain for a water feature on a patio, as well as for a garden pond, check that the spray is suitable.

In windy areas use fountains that produce large water droplets, rather than a fine spray that is blown all over the patio or pond. In extremely windy areas it is best to use fountains that produce a tumbling mass of water.

The height of the spray should not rise to more than half the feature's height, or half the pond's width.

In a pond, the spray must not fall on waterlilies, as it quickly damages their flowers.

When installing a fountain, consult a specialist water garden company to ensure the correct type of pump is used and safely installed.

Solar-powered pumps for small fountains are now available, but they are expensive.

Miniature water gardens

If you do not have the space for a full-scale garden pond, then a quick and easy way to introduce a similarly attractive water feature is to create a miniature water garden in a large tub. When positioned on a patio, a tub water garden can transform an otherwise bare expanse of paving.

Looking after a tub pond

Because tubs and stone sinks hold only a small amount of water, it tends to warm up rapidly in summer and to freeze during winter. For this reason, these features are really only suitable for the summer, and in autumn they should either be emptied or moved into an unheated greenhouse or conservatory.

These miniature water features soon attract the attention of children so, if you have them, for safety reasons it is a good idea to cover any water features with wire-netting.

There is no more satisfying water feature than a full-scale wildlife pond (right), but when space is at a premium a smaller version established in a stone sink can work just as well.

Plants for mini-ponds

There are plenty of good, widely available water plants to choose from, but waterlilies and some other plants should always be selected with care. Some can quickly become excessively large and will dominate the container. They may even suffocate and kill diminutive water plants. Always plant water plants in plastic-mesh baskets; do not put compost in the tub's base and then attempt to set the roots of plants in them.

Waterlilies:

Here is a selection of the most attractive and suitable waterlilies for small water features:

Nymphaea 'Aurora': Flowers first pinkish-yellow, then orange and later red. Attractive leaves splashed brown.

Nymphaea candida: Cup-shaped, white flowers with golden stamens.

Nymphaea 'Graziella': Orange flowers with red stamens. A free-flowering variety.

Nymphaea 'Pygmaea Helvola': Star-shaped, pale yellow flowers with golden stamens. The leaves are mottled in brown.

Nymphaea tetragona (previously known as **N. 'Pygmaea Alba'**): Small, white flowers with yellow stamens.

Marginal plants:

As with any other type of planting, variety is the key to success in planting a miniature water garden. Here are some

Making a tub pond

1 Thoroughly clean the tub in spring or early summer and ensure that the metal bands are strong and secure. Place the tub in position and fill with water; check that it does not leak.

2 If the tub leaks, empty the water and line it with thick, black polythene. Press it into the base and form pleats around the sides. Fill the tub and cut off excess polythene level with the tub's rim.

3 When full of water, the tub can be planted. Position waterlilies on bricks placed on the tub's base, so that leaves float on the surface. As the plants grow, remove one brick at a time.

This combination of an ornate fish and water tumbling onto pebbles works well.

Water tumbling from different levels always creates a pleasing effect.

The decorated back wall of this pebble fountain adds grandeur to the design.

suggestions for widely available marginal plants that will complement waterlilies and enhance any water feature while needing only the minimum of care and attention.

***Carex elata* 'Aurea'** (previously and still popularly known as *C. stricta* **'Bowles' Golden'**): Masses of narrow, golden leaves, about 45cm (1ft) high. Plant it in water about 5cm (2in) deep.

***Schoenoplectus lacustris tabernaemontani* 'Zebrinus'** (but previously and still better known as *Scirpus tabernaemontani* **'Zebrinus'**): This is the zebra rush, with quill-like stems banded in green and white. It grows about 75cm (2ft) high and needs a water depth of 15cm (6in).

Floating water plants:

It is a good idea to intersperse your basic stock of waterlilies and marginal plants with a couple of floating plants. They add an easy charm to any small water feature and are not difficult to find.

***Hydrocharis morsus-ranae* (frog bit):** Bright green leaves; but cut it back often.

***Pistia stratiotes* (water lettuce):** Floating leaves that die down in winter.

Arches, arbours and pergolas are stately garden features that come in a variety of styles, can easily be decorated with plants and are excellent devices for breaking up the garden into different sections, as illustrated here.

Arches, pergolas & arbours

One of the oldest and most popular forms of garden structure is the arch, which has evolved into a larger and more dramatic incarnation known as the pergola. Arches and pergolas originated in Egypt and were later introduced into Italy for supporting vines and straddling paths.

Today, arches and pergolas are standard decorative features of gardens all over the world, being ideal structures for bringing height and permanency to gardens, whether near patios, astride paths or in the centre of a garden. Few sights in the garden are more attractive than an arch or pergola straddling a wide path and decked in flowering climbers or dramatic foliage.

A cousin of the arch and the pergola is the arbour, an equally traditional garden structure originally designed for romantic trysts between lovers. Arbours have featured in the literature of several different cultures for centuries, and remain a timeless garden favourite.

As these structures provide such form and permanence in the garden, it might be assumed that they are enormously costly and time-consuming to construct. Of course, this is the case with the more ambitious types available – and naturally the grander the scale the more materials are required – yet there are arches, pergolas and arbours which can be easily assembled for little expense that will nevertheless make an instant and lasting impact on your garden.

Arches

Apart from straddling paths and separating one part of a garden from another, arches can be positioned against a fence or hedge and a seat positioned between the supporting posts.

Ready-made arches are available to buy from most garden centres, and all you have to do is assemble them. Of course, it is also possible to make your own, and one formed of rustic poles and trellis panels looks attractive, especially in a cottage-garden setting.

Constructing an arch: Use concrete to secure four 10cm (4in) thick and 2.4m (8ft) long rustic poles in the ground; position these posts about 60cm (2ft) apart on either side of a path. Each pole needs to be set 45cm (1½ft) into the ground. Ensure that they are upright, with each having the same length of timber above the ground. Secure cross-timbers to the top, using galvanized nails. Use small nails to secure three pieces of trellis – top and two sides – to the framework.

Pergolas for all gardens

Some pergolas have a clinical nature, others reveal a rustic charm, and this is influenced by the type of material used in their construction. Formal pergolas are ideal for most gardens, but where a cottage-garden ambience is desired, informal designs using rustic poles are more effective.

Traditional-type pergolas: These are made of planed wood, with timber posts 10cm (4in) square and about 2.7m (9ft) high. This gives rigidity when the bottom 60cm (2ft) is concreted into the ground.

A pergola and trellis constructed from rustic poles is relatively cheap and easy to put together. Joints need to be cut with a hand saw or an electric saw, in the manner illustrated below.

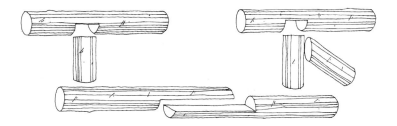

Decorative Garden Features 79

Rustic trellis (illustration page 79)

As an alternative to a rustic pergola, an informal trellis alongside a path and clothed in honeysuckle creates an attractive feature. It is simple to make and demands only modest carpentry skills – here are the joints required.

Securing uprights to horizontals: Create a halving joint by making two cuts, one-third through the horizonal timber and the width of the vertical post apart. Use a sharp chisel to remove the wood; this allows the two timbers to fit snugly. Drill the cross-timber with a 3mm (⅛in) thick wood drill and use a galvanized nail to secure them together.

Securing overlapping horizontal poles: Where the trellis is long, it is inevitable that two or more horizonal poles need to be joined. Choose poles of equal thickness and measure 25cm (10in) from each end. Cut halfway through each timber and then down the centre. Paint the bare wood with a preservative and secure them together with galvanized nails.

Strengthening corners: Rustic poles set at an oblique angle give stability to the corners and are essential for the structure's long life, especially in areas of strong winds. Cut each end of a corner-strengthening pole at a 45-degree angle. To secure it to the framework use galvanized nails; but first drill the wood to prevent it being split by a nail.

Longitudinal timbers rest on the upright posts, themselves supporting cross beams.

Rustic pergolas: These are formed of rustic poles, preferably larch or chestnut; uprights need to be 10cm (4in) thick and 2.7m (9ft) long, so that about 60cm (2ft) can be secured in the ground. Cross timbers need be only 7.5cm (3in) thick.

Romantic arbours

Secluded, shaded but cosily warm arbours help engender romance in gardens, especially when clothed in scented, flowering or leafy plants.

Flowering plants for arbours

There are many richly scented flowering climbers to choose from and several are featured on pages 50 and 51.

Some flowering climbers have a formal appearance and are best grown on relatively sharply-outlined arbours, perhaps constructed from a combination of planed wood supports and square trellis-work. Arbours formed of rustic poles demand informal climbers. However, whatever their nature they must create a screen of foliage.

Formal climbers: These include the ever reliable *Clematis montana* (mountain clematis). It has a deciduous nature, being late coming into leaf in spring but often retaining its leaves until mid-winter, especially in warm and sheltered places. The flowers reveal a formal and regular nature, each with four large petals. The species has white flowers, whereas 'Elizabeth' is soft pink.

Informal climbers: Few climbers are as sprawling and informal as the glorious honeysuckles. *Lonicera periclymenum* 'Belgica' (early Dutch honeysuckle) and *L. p.* 'Serotina' (late Dutch honeysuckle) are described on page 45, but there are others to consider.

Lonicera tragophylla is vigorous and deciduous and only suitable for large arbours, but it has the virtue of growing in shaded areas, where its roots are kept cool and moist. Large, terminal clusters of bright yellow flowers appear during early and mid-summer.

Companion planting on arbours

Growing several climbers on the same arch is an exciting and different way of getting the best from a garden – and if you pick the right ones, it will not take long. Also, plants can be positioned around the base of the arbour to help increase its beauty and impact.

Plant the deciduous *Clematis macropetala*, with nodding, light and dark blue flowers during late spring and early summer, on one side of an arbour, with *Jasminum officinale* (common white jasmine) on the other. The jasmine reveals masses of white flowers in lax clusters from

Arches like this one are very effective when used to extend visual perspectives in the garden. Again, a structure such as this is not time-consuming or costly to build, and it can be clothed in a fast-growing climber in no time at all.

early summer to autumn. Take care that the vigorous jasmine does not swamp the more reserved growth of the clematis. Plant lavender on each side of the arbour.

Plant a dark-petalled, large-flowered clematis on either side of an entrance to an arbour covered in the bright yellowish-green-leaved, herbaceous plant *Humulus lupulus* 'Aureus' (yellow-leaved hop). Use clematis varieties such as 'Vyvyan Pennell' (violet-purple flushed carmine), 'Lasurstern' (purple-blue) or 'Lord Nevill' (deep purple-blue). For a less dramatic picture, use 'Lady Caroline Nevill', which reveals lavender-grey flowers with mauve stripes.

Coniferous entrance to an arbour

An unusual and very attractive entrance to an arbour can be created by planting two large, yellow-leaved conifers planted about 1.8m (6ft) apart. Although it will take some time for the conifers to reach their full height and burgeon with dense growth, once they get there, an entrance gap can be trimmed through their foliage without too much difficulty, creating an instantly atractive feature. Use fast-growing conifers such as *Chamaecyparis lawsoniana* 'Lutea' or *C. l.* 'Lane' (previously known as 'Lanei'). A wooden arbour can be positioned behind the conifers as soon as they are large enough to shield it.

Seats & benches to improve all gardens

One obvious and immediate way to enhance your garden is to place attractive garden furniture all around it. However, you could quickly run up a very large bill buying everything from the local garden centre. What better than to make your own bench, tailored to suit your garden? The following features are not difficult to construct and require only modest carpentry skills and a little knowledge of brick-laying.

Wooden seats

These come in a variety of different forms; some are just a stout plank secured to brick or wood supports, while others are tailored for specific places.

Tree seat: This is ideal for constructing around a large tree. It can be combined with a paved area formed around the tree, or located in a more relaxed setting such as a woodland or wildflower garden.

The construction of a tree seat appears more complicated than it is; four (sometimes five when encircling a large tree) frame-like supports are needed, with 10cm (4in) wide and 2.5cm (1in) thick planks screwed to their tops to form a seat.

Rustic bench seat: This is quickly and easily made by digging two holes, each about 30cm (12in) wide and 45cm (18in) deep, 1.2m (4ft) apart. Thick logs, about 20cm (8in) wide and 60cm (2ft) long, are inserted 45cm (18in) into the soil, with coarse rubble rammed around them. First, however, check that their tops are level. Then, use several galvanized nails to secure the plank to the supports.

Formal bench seat: Ideal for a formal setting, perhaps at the edge of a patio or terrace. This bench needs wood-working and modest brick-laying skills. About 1.2m (4ft) apart, construct two pillars, 23cm square (slightly less if metric bricks are used), and about 38cm (15in) high. Use masonry fixings to secure a 36mm (1½in) thick, 20–23cm (8–9in) long and 5–7.5cm (2–3in) wide piece

---

All boxed in

Planting and clipping the small-leaved, evergreen shrub *Buxus sempervirens*, the common box, to form the back and arms of a 1.5–1.8m (5–6ft) long concrete bench creates an unusual yet attractive feature.

Alternatively, use a thick and wide piece of wood to create the bench; it produces a more natural feature than concrete and is warmer to sit on.

Position the bench and plant young plants 30–38cm (12–15in) apart in a line 30cm (12in) from the bench's back and sides. After planting, prune off the upper one-third of shoots to encourage bushiness. Several subsequent hard clippings – each less than the last – will be needed during the first few years to create dense and attractive growth.

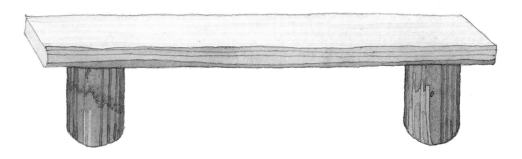

of wood to each plinth. The seating strips, 36–50mm (1–2in) thick and 6.5cm (2in) wide, can then be screwed to the top. Preferably, the ends should extend beyond each plinth by about 10cm (4in). Paint the wood white, using several coats.

Concrete and brick seats

Concrete and brick seats bring different textures and effects to the garden and can be constructed to any individually-tailored plan. However, they will usually take slightly longer to construct than wooden seats.

Brick planter and seat: This is an attractive and relatively easily-built feature, formed of a brick planter about 90cm (3ft) square and 75cm (2ft) high. The centre is open, with drainage gaps left between several bricks in the base. The base is filled with coarse drainage material, then top-soil in which plants can be placed.

The seat part is made of a brick base, four courses high and about 30cm (12in) wide; one or two paving slabs cemented to the bricks form the actual seat.

This attractive seat/planter combination does not require any great skill to build. It does not matter if your cement joints are uneven or your bricks not completely straight: part of the design's charm is its rustic irregularity.

Quick & easy scree gardens

Rock gardens are expensive and time-consuming to construct, but you can swiftly bring the distinctive flavour of alpine plants to your garden by making a scree bed. It is so much easier and cheaper to make than a rock garden, yet a scree garden still enables small bulbous plants, miniature conifers and dwarf rock garden plants to be grown with ease.

Choosing the site

If a rock garden is already in existence, position the scree bed at its base, so that it appears to be a natural extension, spreading out into a mushroom shape at its end. Alternatively, create a scree by the side of a path.

The essentials for a successful gravel garden are:
- a sunny site away from overhanging trees
- well-drained soil
- an area free from perennial weeds
- no wire-worms, cockchafer larvae or other soil pests.

A windbreak, perhaps formed of conifers, helps to protect alpine plants from cold winds.

Simple scree gardens bring instant, easily-manageable variety to the garden floor, and will look good for years.

Peat beds for woodland plants

Peat beds are ideal places for growing acid-loving woodland plants. Instead of being formed of rocks, peat beds are made out of peat blocks used in a similar manner to create stratified layers.

Peat blocks can also be used to form a low wall around the feature, although on steep slopes old railway sleepers or planks nailed to stout upright posts often work better, as they are less likely to fall away from the peat bed.

Plants to consider using in peat beds include astilbe, azalea, cassiope, dodecatheon, gaultheria, some primulas and autumn-flowering gentians.

Constructing a scree bed

The quick and easy way to build an alpine scree bed in your garden.

1 Dig out the area to 38cm (15in) deep and fill the base with 15cm (6in) of clean rubble. Ensure the roots of perennial weeds have been removed. Spread sharp sand over the rubble, forming a layer 5cm (2in) thick.

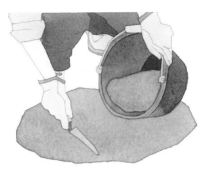

2 Over the sand spread a 15cm (6in) thick layer of compost, formed of one part clean topsoil, one of moist peat, and three of sharp grit.

3 Position a few rocks so that they appear to be natural outcrops. These help to give the scree bed height and permanency.

4 Firm the compost and plant a range of alpines. Then, carefully form a 2.5cm (1in) thick layer of 6mm (¼in) shingle or chippings over the surface.

Below: Plants for scree beds range from miniature bulbs to mat-forming and flowering perennials.

Plants for scree beds

Aethionema 'Warley Rose' (Persian candytuft): Evergreen perennial with deep rose flowers during late spring and early summer.
Height: 10–15cm (4–5in)
Spread: 30–38cm (12–15in)
Chionodoxa luciliae (glory of the snow): Light-blue, white-centred flowers during late winter and early spring.

Height: 15cm (6in)
Plant: 7.5cm (3in) apart
Crocus chrysanthus: Golden-yellow, goblet-shaped flowers during late winter and early spring. Also, white, blue and purple forms.
Height: 7.5–10cm (3–4in)
Plant: 7.5cm (3in) apart
Ipheion uniflorum (spring starflower): Clump-forming, with

white to violet-blue flowers during mid and late spring.
Height: 15–20cm (6–8in)
Plant: 7.5cm (3in) apart
Penstemon laetus roezlii (previously known as *P. roezlii*): Low, spreading, evergreen with tubular, lavender to violet-blue flowers during mid-summer.
Height: 10–20cm (4–8in)
Spread: 30–38cm (12–15in)

Raised beds

Informal raised beds are ideal for bringing 'height' to a garden, where they create attractive focal points as well as enabling plants to be grown at waist-height so that they can be easily seen and tended. Once again, they can be surprisingly quick, easy and economical to construct, and they will repay the initial effort with many years of eye-catching service, if planted up and regularly maintained.

Above: The way a raised bed is planted dictates its ultimate efficacy as a garden feature. As always, variety is the key – tall, shapely plants will provide enhanced verticality, low, sprawling plants will give the bed width and depth.

This is also a good way to grow rock garden plants in areas where the soil is too acid or exceptionally alkaline – you have to fill the raised bed, so use the soil of your choice.

Economic construction

A cheaper alternative to constructing a raised bed from expensive stones is to use reconstituted stone blocks, railway sleepers or old, strong timbers.

To ensure the long life of a raised bed, it must be soundly constructed; if stones are used, dig trenches 20–30cm (8–12in) where the walls are to be positioned. Form and compact a 5–10cm (2–4in) thick layer of clean rubble, then lay a 10cm (4in) thick base of concrete. Be sure to leave drainage gaps or holes in the concrete base to enable the bed to drain freely. If railway sleepers are used, the layer of concrete is not needed.

When the walls are complete, fill the inside one-third deep with clean rubble, again, leaving drainage gaps between the stones, then top up with friable, weed-free topsoil. A good depth of soil or growing medium is between 30cm (1ft) and 45cm (1½ft), ideally placed over a water-permeable woven plastic membrane that separates it from the layer of drainage rubble. Allow the soil to settle before putting the plants in position. Be prepared to add further soil to 'top up' the bed and bring the surface to a level fractionally below the edges.

Creating height in low raised beds

In order for your raised bed to exert the maximum visual influence on your garden, it must be genuinely 'raised'. Far too many beds lack impact because they have been set too low in the first place and then planted up unimaginatively.

If you use a combination of tall and low plants in lots of different colours, you can overcome this common problem quickly and easily and create really effective height and colour, wherever the bed is positioned. Here is one highly effective arrangement to consider:

Plant a group of two or three small, upright, evergreen conifers such as *Juniperus communis* 'Compressa', 75–90cm (2–3ft) apart. Around these form a sea of lower-growing plants, such as *Arabis procurrens* 'Variegata' (previously known as *Arabis ferdinandi-coburgi* 'Variegata'), which is mat-forming with dark green leaves splashed with silver. Thyme creates an impressive background, when used in conjunction with these tall and mat-forming plants; use *Thymus serpyllum*, in a range of colours from red, through pink to white. Be bold in your selection of colours, for added interest. Additionally, plant *Potentilla neumanniana* (previously known as *P. tabernaemontani*, and popularly as spring cinquefoil), with bright yellow flowers.

By restricting a raised bed's width to 1.5m (5ft) and its height to 60cm (2ft), it is possible to reach all the plants, even from a wheelchair.

Plants to clothe the sides of a raised bed

Plants with a tumbling and trailing nature soon clothe the sides of raised beds. They can be planted along the top edge of the bed, so that they cascade down the sides, or put into gaps left in the sides.

Asperula arcadiensis (previously known as **A. suberosa**, and popularly as alpine woodruff): Alpine perennial, with white, hairy leaves and shell-pink flowers during early and mid-summer. It is best planted at the top of a wall, where it helps to cloak the edge.

Aubrieta deltoidea: Low-growing and trailing evergreen perennial with hoary-green leaves and masses of cross-shaped, purple to rose-lilac flowers during spring and early summer. After flowering, cut back the foliage to encourage a second flush of flowers in autumn. There are several varieties; one has gold-variegated leaves.

Aurina saxatilis (previously known as **Alyssum saxatile**, and popularly as gold dust): Evergreen, shrubby perennial with grey-green leaves and golden-yellow flowers from mid-spring to early summer.

Erinus alpinus (fairy foxglove): Evergreen perennial with mid-green leaves and masses of bright pink, star-like flowers from spring to late summer.

Helianthemum nummularium (rock rose): Hardy evergreen shrub with deep green leaves and saucer-shaped flowers during early and mid-summer.

Phlox subulata (moss phlox): Sub-shrubby and forming large mats of mid-green leaves smothered in purple or pink flowers during spring. There are several varieties.

Paved surfaces

Paved surfaces have the ability to enhance an entire garden. Of course, the choice of materials is entirely personal, but as they form the main leisure areas around houses they are certain to be noticed. Before constructing a patio, have a look at the wide range available, at garden centres, in neighbouring gardens and in magazines, to ensure you make the right choice for your garden.

The range of materials used in the construction of patios and other paved surfaces is incredibly diverse, and while some have a clinical nature others offer a varied and informal appearance. Materials can be mixed with one another to create a more attractive surface, as well as to direct where people walk in your garden.

Paving materials

Some paving materials are very expensive, but remember that a patio or terrace formed of hard-wearing and attractive materials will remain functional, interesting and a pleasure to use for thirty or more years. Materials to consider include:

Concrete slabs: These range in thickness from 42–50mm (1–2in) and the most common size is 45cm (1½ft) square; there are quarter and half-slabs, so that patterns can be created.

Plain slabs 60cm (2ft) square and 75cm (2½ft) by 60cm (2ft) are available, but these are difficult to handle. The surfaces of paving slabs range from smooth to riven, while some have designs that allow them to create larger patterns.

Hexagonal and round slabs: These usually have smooth or slightly rough surfaces; the hexagonal stones can be laid in patterns, while round ones can be used as stepping stones in a sea of irregular-shaped materials, such as pebbles.

Granite setts: Often expensive, but hard-wearing and ideal for using in limited amounts to create variations of shape and texture.

Brick pavers: Hard-wearing and usually laid on a thick bed of sharp sand to create so-called 'flexible paving'. The 'flexibility' arises from the fact that the pavers can be lifted and later replaced if it turns out that repairs to cables and pipes below them are necessary.

Natural stone: These have an irregular size, shape and thickness and are ideal for creating a natural-looking surface in informal gardens. However, natural stone is expensive.

Cobbles: These are attractive but best reserved for use with other materials.

Opposite: It is easy to enhance paving by leaving gaps between the pavers. Once the surface is complete, plants can be set between the stones.

Designing with cobbles

Use cobbles to create areas where you do not want people to walk. For example, where casement windows open outwards on to a paved area, a 38–45cm (15–18in) wide strip of cobbles will deter people from walking close to the building and bumping into an open window. Additionally, plants in large tubs can be placed on them to prevent people walking too close and damaging the flowers.

Decorative Garden Features

Renewing gates & fences

Removing an old gate or fence and replacing it with a new one can have a dramatic effect on a garden. By the same token, re-painting a fence can improve the whole surrounding aspect.

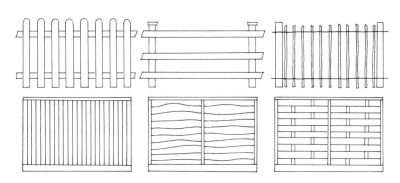

Fences tend to be chosen both for their functionality and their aestheticism. Obviously a closed style acts as a more effective screen.

New fences for old

The range of different fences now available is extremely wide; a few of them are shown here. Several fences, such as ranch-style and spike-chain fencing, have a modern, open style, whereas solid fencing creates a blocked-off effect that lends itself well to older-style properties.

Picket fencing has a cottage-garden feel to it, as well as a 'colonial' appearance, and can look very appealing. Additionally, it can be 'personalized' by shaping the tops of individual palings (see box below).

Brick boundary walls are not always as long-lived as one might think; their durability much depends on the depth and detailed preparation of their foundations. Also, where the tops of walls are left bare and uncapped, water will soon permeate the bricks; frost is then able to cause further damage.

The following ideas will help you extend the life of existing fences and walls or improve your garden altogether by suggesting replacements.

Extending the life of a fence

Whatever type of material you use for your fence, in relative terms it will be expensive. If you follow these tips, it will last longer and look better in the garden:
● When installing posts, ensure they are upright and that the top of the concrete holding them in place is smooth and at an angle that sheds water away from the post.
● Use pressure-treated wooden posts

Personalizing picket fences

Picket fences are always attractive if well constructed and maintained, but you could go one step better by personalizing yours. Cut the top of each paling to a shape that appeals to you, and your fence will immediately stand out. There are four basic shapes that are easy to cut into a paling (see below).

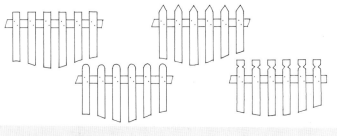

Squared-off paling   **Pointed paling**
      Rounded paling   **Waisted paling**

impregnated with rot-resistant chemicals.

● Do not allow the bases of fencing panels to rest on the soil. Preferably, there should be a gap of 5–7.5cm (2–3in).

● Use only galvanized nails to secure fencing panels to posts. If ordinary nails are used, they rust, and during storms the entire panel may break away from the post and be smashed.

● Nail wooden caps to the tops of wooden posts to prevent water entering the wood. Alternatively, cut the tops of posts at an angle.

● Paint fences with wood preservatives. Coat both sides of the fence and ensure that preservative reaches into joints.

● Regularly clear away soil, debris and plants from the bases of fences; if left, it encourages wood to decay.

Gates for all gardens

Well-proportioned gates that harmonize with a house and garden always enhance a property and its value. There are many types of gate to choose from, in both single and double styles. Gates are nearly always made out of either wood or metal.

Wood is the most adaptable of materials and can be used to create many styles in gates; some have an open and slatted nature, while others are close-boarded. Those constructed of soft woods are usually painted, while hardwood types require oiling or varnishing.

The joints on old wooden gates eventually become loose, although the wood usually remains sound. Apart from taking the gate apart and re-gluing the joints, metal angle-brackets can be quickly screwed into place to hold the wood together.

Metal gates are usually made of wrought-iron, which lasts for many years. Their shapes are varied and some have a highly ornate appearance; avoid using very ornate types in plain gardens.

A coating of paint every few years extends the gate's life and improves its appearance.

Driveway gates are by definition large, prominent features. Choose a style that is in keeping with the nature of your house and garage and that ties in well with other garden furniture.

Three popular styles of gate: a classic wrought-iron garden gate, a tall wrought-iron terrace gate and a standard wooden picket gate.

Safe-guarding a gate

When installing a new, wrought-iron gate – an expensive item that will always look good and attract attention – position the top hinge in a downward direction, and the lower one upwards to support the gate's weight. This helps to prevent the gate being easily lifted off its hinges and stolen. Installing a coiled spring that helps close the gate also deters thieves.

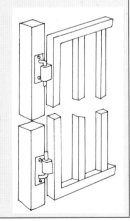

Painting with Plants

Gardens offer a broad canvas for gardeners to paint, and within most of them there are opportunities to introduce new features and to group plants in exciting and colourful combinations. This chapter examines a wide range of features, from nosegay borders to Japanese and winter-flowering gardens. The flower arranger's garden offers a wide range of flowers that are suitable for cutting to display in vases indoors. Other colourful features are foliage plants that create a long-term display, and choosing groups of seed-raised plants that each year brighten borders with ever-changing colours.

Companion planting will create exciting displays throughout the year and offers the opportunity to get the very best from plants. It also helps to extend the period when plants are most attractive. The following combinations offer a plethora of ideas for strong colour combinations, even in autumn and winter.

Autumn-coloured leaves

Many deciduous shrubs and trees have leaves that create the most spectacular displays in autumn, and there are a few which also produce exciting flowers.

Cercidiphyllum japonicum: Elegant tree, with rich green leaves that assume red and yellow tints in autumn.
Height: 6–7.5m (20–25ft)
Spread: 4.5–6m (15–20ft)

Cornus florida (flowering dogwood): Hardy, well-branched shrub or small tree with dark green leaves that turn brilliant shades of scarlet and orange in autumn.
Height: 3–4.5m (10–15ft)
Spread: 3–5.4m (10–18ft)

Enkianthus campanulatus: Upright shrub with finely-toothed, green leaves that turn brilliant red in autumn. Clusters of creamy-white, bell-shaped flowers appear in late spring.
Height: 1.8–2.4m (6–8ft)
Spread: 1–1.5m (3–5ft)

Fothergilla major: Slow-growing shrub with sweetly-scented, bottle-brush-like white flowers in late spring. In autumn, the dark green leaves assume rich red and orange-yellow tints.
Height: 1.8–2.4m (6–8ft)
Spread: 1.5–1.8m (5–6ft)

Hamamelis mollis 'Pallida' (Chinese witch hazel): Shrub or small tree with golden-yellow, spider-like flowers in winter and leaves that turn yellow in autumn.
Height: 1.8–2.4m (6–8ft)
Spread: 1.8–2.4m (6–8ft)

Hydrangea paniculata: Large, spreading shrub with mid-green leaves that assume yellow shades in autumn. Additionally, it bears massed heads of white flowers.
Height: 2.4–3m (8–10ft)
Spread: 2.4–3m (8–10ft)

Liquidambar styraciflua (sweet gum): Hardy, pyramidal tree with maple-like leaves that turn rich orange and scarlet in autumn. It creates a superb focal point in a large lawn.
Height: 5.4–6m (18–20ft)
Spread: 2.4–3.6m (8–12ft)

Malus tschonoskii: An erect, pyramidal tree with single, white, pink-tinted, flowers in late spring and early summer. During autumn, the mid-green leaves turn red and yellow. Position it towards the end of a garden, so that it creates a focal point in autumn.
Height: 6–9m (20–30ft)
Spread: 2.4–3m (8–10ft)

Rhus typhina (stag's horn sumach): A spreading and suckering shrub with mid-green leaves formed of many leaflets that assume rich orange-red, purple and yellow tints in autumn. It can be planted in a border to create autumn colour.
Height: 2–4–3.6m (8–12ft)
Spread: 3–3.6m (10–12ft)

For the imaginative gardener, the garden is just like a huge canvas, waiting to be painted. Colourful plants offer the greatest natural palette of all.

Great planting combinations

Gardens comprise a medley of plants, from herbaceous perennials to shrubs, trees, annuals, biennials, bulbs, ferns and grasses. They look good on their own, but when planted in attractive groups they are even better.

Selecting plants that form attractive partnerships with each other requires careful thought. For example, if they are flowering plants they must create their displays at the same time. Equally, one plant should not dominate and eventually suffocate its neighbour. There are many exciting combinations of plants and by choosing them carefully 'mix-and-match' displays can be created throughout the year.

In spring

● Plant the bulbous, blue-flowered *Muscari armeniacum* (grape hyacinth) in large drifts under the deciduous, slow-growing tree *Magnolia stellata* (star magnolia) which bears white, star-like, fragrant flowers.
● Plant purple-blue forms of the bulbous, large-flowered Dutch crocuses around the deciduous shrub *Ribes sanguineum* 'King Edward VII' (flowering currant), with deep crimson flowers.
● Plant golden forms of Dutch crocuses around the evergreen shrub *Ribes laurifolium*, which bears pendent, greenish-yellow flowers. This combination is ideal for a large rock garden.
● Plant the bulbous, sky-blue-flowered *Chionodoxa sardensis* (glory of the snow) around the white-flowered Rhododendron 'Bric-à-brac' Group. This arrangement is also ideal for a rock garden.

Early summer

● In a corner of a woodland garden plant the fragrant, yellow–flowered *Rhododendron luteum* with a sea of bluebells in front.
● Plant the rose–purple flowered *Erica australis* (Spanish heath) in front of the yellow-flowered *Ulex europaeus* 'Plenus' (gorse). This is an ideal arrangement where the gorse is used as a boundary.
● Plant hardy, dwarf, deciduous azaleas in colours including red, pink, apricot and orange under the outer extremes of the branches of the yellow-flowered, deciduous tree, *Laburnum anagyroides* (golden rain).

Mid-summer

● Plant the bulbous *Lilium candidum* (Madonna lily), with white, trumpet–shaped flowers and golden pollen, with the hardy biennial *Digitalis purpurea* (foxglove). The addition of *Meconopsis cambrica* (Welsh poppy), a hardy perennial with bright-

Coloured berries

Berries bring a variation on the theme of colour to gardens. Trees and shrubs that provide them include:
● *Callicarpa bodinieri giraldii* (beauty bush): Deciduous shrub with round, deep lilac to violet-blue berries in autumn.
● *Gaultheria mucronata* (previously known as *Pernettya mucronata*): Clusters of berries in autumn, in colours including rose, pink, white, purple and red.
● *Pyracantha* 'Watereri' (firethorn): Bright red berries from autumn to early spring. Other species and varieties have berries in orange-red, rich yellow and orange.
● *Sorbus* 'Joseph Rock': Creamy-yellow berries, maturing to amber, in autumn.

yellow, poppy-like flowers, adds further colour to the display.

● For a white-and-silver display, plant the bulbous, white-flowered *Lilium regale* among the hardy herbaceous perennial *Artemisia ludoviciana*, which reveals white leaves.

● Plant the deciduous shrub *Hydrangea arborescens* 'Grandiflora', with pure-white flowers borne in large, rounded clusters, in front of a hedge of *Taxus baccata* (yew). The dark green foliage of the yew highlights the hydrangea's flowers.

Late summer

● Plant the hardy herbaceous perennial *Salvia × superba*, with tall spires of rich, purple-blue flowers, in front of the bulbous *Lilium henryi*, with pale, apricot-yellow flowers with red spots.

● For a white-and-silver display, plant *Yucca flaccida* 'Ivory', with white, bell-shaped flowers

and a distinctive 'architectural' appearance, in a sea of the silver-leaved *Senecio cineraria* 'White Diamond' or 'Silver Dust' (previously known as *Cineraria maritima*).

Autumn

● Plant the late-flowering *Clematis flammula*, a bushy and deciduous type with pure-white, sweetly-scented flowers to cover a low arch or trellis, with the herbaceous perennial *Aconitum carmichaelii* in front. This monkshood (previously and still better known as *A. wilsonii*) displays pyramids of amethyst-blue flowers. 'Barker's Variety' has deep blue flowers.

● Plant *Sedum spectabile* (ice plant), which has pink flowers that assume a mauve tinge in autumn, with the bulbous *Colchicum speciosum* (autumn crocus). This crocus has rose-purple, goblet-shaped flowers that appear before its leaves.

Painting with Plants   **95**

Roses as companions

For many years, roses have been grown on their own, in beds or trained along walls, but to make better use of space, as well as to create more interesting displays, they can be mixed superbly well with other plants.

Mix and matching shrub roses

Plant the species rose *Rosa banksiae* 'Lutea' (Lady Banks's rose), which bears clusters of double, yellow flowers in late spring and early summer, where they contrast with the fragrant, mauve flowers of the deciduous climber *Wisteria sinensis* (Chinese wisteria).

Position the Modern Shrub Rose 'Nevada', with semi-double, creamy-white flowers, where blue-flowered delphiniums and campanulas can be mingled with it.

The Hybrid Musk 'Buff Beauty', with warm, apricot-yellow flowers borne in large trusses, looks superb when surrounded by light-blue, white and light-orange flowers. These can be provided by the lavender-blue flowered *Nepeta* × *faassenii* (catmint) and *Papaver orientale* 'Perry's White', a form of the Oriental poppy.

Cohabiting bush roses

Plant the pale yellow Hybrid Tea 'Grandpa Dickson' against a background of the deciduous *Berberis thunbergii* 'Atropurpurea', which has dark purple leaves. For added colour, plant a collar of the half-hardy annual *Nicotiana alata* 'Lime Green', which has yellow-green flowers.

The buttercup-yellow Floribunda 'Allgold' creates an exciting feature when planted with the large-flowered *Clematis* 'Countess of Lovelace'. It has deep lavender flowers from early summer to autumn; double flowers appear in summer, while single types show in late summer and into autumn.

Plant the vigorous Floribunda 'Queen Elizabeth', with cyclamen-pink flowers, against a background of a hedge formed of *Taxus baccata* (yew). The yew's dark green leaves highlight the rose's flowers.

Companions for ramblers and climbers

Plant the modern climber 'New Dawn', with silvery blush-pink flowers, so that the vigorous *Clematis* 'Perle d'Azure' can climb through it. This clematis has blue flowers.

Position the rambler 'Bobbie James', with semi-double, creamy-white flowers, to clamber over a pergola or into a tree. Plant the hardy herbaceous perennial *Nepeta* × *faassenii* (catmint) around its base. It produces whorls of lavender-blue flowers from early summer to early autumn.

Opposite:
A magnificent rose-covered trellis arch, in all its summer glory. The climbing roses contrast beautifully with the bright red paeonies in the foreground.

Ground-covering roses

Beds positioned alongside patios especially benefit from ground-covering roses, but do not expect them to prevent the growth of weeds. Rather, they create a magnificent blanket of colour.

The County Series of roses is popular for creating colour at ground level. Most of them grow 30–45cm (12–18in) high and with a 60cm–1.2m (2–4ft) spread. There are several varieties, including:

'Avon': Pearly-white	'Norfolk': Bright yellow
'Essex': Rich reddish-pink	'Suffolk': Bright crimson-scarlet
Hampshire': Glowing scarlet	'Warwickshire': Deep rosy-red
'Hertfordshire': Carmine-pink	'Wiltshire': Deep rosy-pink

Flower corners from seed

With the opportunity to create a wide range of colours each year, it is difficult to understand why flower borders formed of hardy annuals are not more popular. It is true that these beds involve quite a lot of work, in relative terms, but this pales into insignificance when you see the superb results and gain the opportunity each year to experiment with new varieties and their positions within a border.

Opposite: This vibrant display of hardy annuals grown from seed is dominated by *Rudbeckia* 'Autumn Leaves'.

Do not underestimate the power of these plants! Yes, they do take a little more work than most – there is digging to be done in winter, soil preparation in spring, seeds to be sown, seedlings to be thinned, and so on – but nevertheless they will bring superb results to your garden very quickly and you will have great fun re-arranging your groups of annuals over the years. The seed companies produce countless different varieties each growing season, so you will never have to look very hard in order to come up with new ideas for visual effects in your borders. Here are some classic colour combinations:

Annual grasses

These introduce shape and texture variations to borders, and are ideal for filling gaps around existing plants. Preferably, they like well-drained, fertile soil in full sun.
- *Agrostis nebulosa* (cloud grass): Tufted and wispy, to about 38cm (15in) high. It combines well with the hardy annual *Echium lycopsis* (purple viper's bugloss).
- *Hordeum jubatum* (squirrel grass): Soft, plume-like, light-green heads about 45cm (1½ft) high. It cohabits well with dimorphothecas.
- *Lagurus ovatus* (hare's-tail grass): Fluffy, white flowers about 30cm (1ft) high. Grow it with the hardy annual *Clarkia elegans*.

Groups of annuals to consider

Mainly yellow: For a principally yellow annual border, sow yellow-flowered annual lupins in front of *Helianthus annuus* (sunflower), which reveals large, yellow flowers with brown or purple centres. To create a striking colour contrast, sow the crimson-flowered *Amaranthus caudatus* (love-lies-bleeding) on either side.

Pink, scarlet and red medley: For brilliant red and pink contrasts, sow two large patches of scarlet annual poppies (*Papaver rhoeas* and popularly known as the field poppy) and red, low-growing nasturtiums (*Tropaeolum majus*) at the front of the border, with the pink-flowered *Agrostemma githago* 'Milas' in a large, kidney-shaped area behind both of them.

Cottage-garden corners: Mixed annual borders are ideally suited to cottage gardens, so try a medley of *Malcolmia maritima* (Virginian stock), *Iberis umbellata* (candytuft) and *Clarkia pulchella*.

The Virginian stock has sweetly-scented, cross-shaped flowers in white, pink, red, lavender and purple; candytuft has clustered heads of white, red, or purple flowers; clarkia bears dainty sprays of flowers in white, crimson, or violet.

A scented and pastel-shaded study: Sow *Matthiola bicornis* (night-scented stock) in a group with the silver-leaved border plant *Stachys byzantina* (lamb's tongue), the half-hardy *Nicotiana alata* 'Dwarf White Bedder' and the hardy biennial *Dianthus barbatus* 'Giant White'. As well as having a delicate and subdued appearance, this group of plants produces a range of scents that are an absolute feast for the nose! **Brightening a low wall:** Where a low wall borders a garden, sow a trailing form of *Tropaeolum majus* (nasturtium) to sprawl over the top and to mingle with shrubs such as *Cotoneaster horizontalis*, a deciduous shrub with branches that have a herringbone appearance. The cotoneaster offers the bonus of bearing thick clusters of round, red berries, for added effect.

When sowing hardy annuals

Dig the soil in winter. In spring, systematically tread over it; then, rake the surface level.

Mark the area into sections, one for each variety. Use a pointed stick to form drills 6–12mm (¼–½in) deep and 23cm (9in) apart.

Form the drills within each section at 45 degrees to their neighbours.

Sow seeds thinly; ensure the seeds fall in the drill's base.

Use the back of a metal rake to draw soil over the seeds, then firm by pressing with the rake's head.

If birds are a problem, place twiggy sticks over the drills. Alternatively, stretch cottons 10cm (4in) above the surface, but ensure birds are not harmed by them.

Nosegay gardens

Fragrant plants are always welcome in gardens and many scented plants are featured throughout this book. Nosegay gardens, however, are something special and a little different – ideal for introducing a wide range of rich fragrances to beds alongside patios.

In earlier years, nosegay beds were parts of medicinal herb gardens, at a time when a nosegay was a bunch of sweetly smelling herbs. Nowadays, 'nosegay bed' is a term given to a herb garden with scented plants.

Rich fragrances

Some herbs release fragrance through their flowers, others through their leaves, stems and seeds. There are many fragrant herbs to choose from, including:

Lavandula angustifolia (English lavender): Evergreen shrub with aromatic foliage and fragrant flowers, which when dried are used in pot-pourris. It has been grown for many centuries and was formerly used in elixirs that were claimed to cure anything from swooning fits to vertigo and loss of memory.

Lavandula stoechas (French lavender): Evergreen shrub, slightly less hardy than English lavender, with distinctive purple-tufted flower tops during early and mid-summer.

Aloysia triphylla (but previously known as *Lippia citriodora* (lemon-scented verbena): Slightly tender deciduous shrub with strongly lemon-scented leaves when crushed.

Convallaria majalis (lily of the valley): Herbaceous perennial with creeping rhizomes and roots. Arching stems bear bell-shaped, waxy-white flowers in spring. It can be an invasive plant and will penetrate loose brickwork.

Reseda odorata (mignonette): Hardy annual with orange-yellow flowers throughout summer and often into autumn. As well as being used in nosegays, it was held in great esteem by lovers: an old saying suggests that good fortune accompanies a lover who thrice rolls in a bed of mignonette!

Calendula officinalis (pot marigold): Hardy annual with daisy-like flowers, usually bright yellow or orange. Both the foliage and flowers have a pungent aroma.

Rosmarinus officinalis (rosemary): Evergreen shrub with leaves that emit a rich, aromatic, slightly camphor-like bouquet. When preparing rosemary for room decoration, hammer the stem ends and place overnight in cold water in a cool, still room. Years ago, an old saying claimed that 'where rosemary flourishes, the woman rules'.

Scabiosa atropurpurea (sweet scabious): Hardy annual with sweetly-fragrant dark crimson or purple flowers borne on long stems from mid-summer to autumn. When cut, the flowers last a week or more before the petals drop.

Afternoon delight

The four o'clock plant (*Mirabilis jalapa*) regularly opens its fragrant, trumpet-shaped flowers in late afternoon. The flowers – in various colours including yellow, red, crimson, rose and white – fade during the following morning. It is a tender perennial, usually grown as a half-hardy annual and best suited to warm, sunny and wind-sheltered corners.

Here, in this attractive border, the gorgeously fragrant lemon balm competes with thyme and marigolds for attention.

Evening fragrance under windows

Small flowerbeds under windows are ideal places for sowing a combination of the hardy annuals Virginian stock (*Malcolmia maritima*) and the night-scented stock (*Matthiola bicornis*).

The Virginian stock grows about 20cm (8in) high, with red, yellow, white and lilac flowers that appear about four weeks after sowing seeds during spring and early summer in drills 6mm (¼in) deep and 15cm (6in) apart. Thin seedlings to 15cm (6in) apart.

The night-scented stock grows 30–38cm (12–15in) high, with purple-lilac flowers that open at night and saturate the air with a rich scent. Sow seeds in patches with the Virginian stock, in drills 6mm (¼in) deep and 20cm (8in) apart. Thin seedlings 20–23cm (8–9in) apart.

Fragrant pots

Fragrant plants in containers create height and shape variations in nosegay gardens. Choose containers that have an old and ornate style.

Try *Chamaemelum nobile* (chamomile), a perennial, with a mat-forming nature, formed of finely-dissected, mid-green leaves that emit a refreshing aromatic bouquet, accompanied by daisy-like white flowers.

Flower arranger's garden

A vase arranged with freshly-cut flowers from the garden immediately brings vitality to indoors. Many annuals and biennials can be used to produce cut-flowers, while shrubs with colourful foliage and berries add permanency to floral displays.

Annuals as cut-flowers

These are either hardy annuals that can be sown in spring where they are to germinate, grow and flower, or half-hardy types raised in gentle warmth in greenhouses in spring and planted outside only when all risk of frost has passed. There are many of these plants to choose from, including:

Callistephus chinensis (**China aster**): Half-hardy annual with large, daisy-like flowers throughout summer.

Calendula officinalis (**pot marigold**): Hardy annual with large, daisy-like, yellow or orange flowers throughout summer.

Clarkia amoena (**satin flower**): Hardy annual, bearing single, double or semi-double flowers in pink, white, cherry-red or salmon during mid- and late summer.

Consolida ajacis (previously known as **Delphinium consolida**, and popularly as **larkspur**): Hardy annual, developing spires of pink, red, purple or white flowers from early to mid-summer.

Gaillardia pulchella (**blanket flower**): Half-hardy annual with large, daisy-like, brightly-faced 5cm (2in) wide flowers from mid-summer to autumn.

Iberis umbellata (**candytuft**): Hardy annual with domed heads of red, purple or white flowers from early to late summer.

Nigella damascena (**love-in-a-mist**): Hardy annual with finely-cut leaves and large, blue or white flowers from early to late summer.

Reseda odorata (**mignonette**): Hardy annual, with yellow-white flowers throughout summer and into autumn.

Schizanthus pinnatus (**butterfly bush**):

Other herbaceous plants as cut-flowers

Agapanthus 'Headbourne Hybrids'
Alstroemeria 'Ligtu Hybrids'
Leucanthemum × superbum (previously known as *Chrysanthemum maximum*, and popularly as Shasta daisy)
Echinops ritro (globe thistle)
Lupins 'Russell Strain'
Lysimachia punctata (yellow loosestrife)
Phlox paniculata
Scabiosa caucasica (pincushion flower)
Zantedeschia aethiopica 'Crowborough'

Other annuals as cut-flowers

Amaranthus caudatus (love-lies-bleeding) – hardy annual.
Coreopsis tinctoria (tickseed) – hardy annual
Cosmos bipinnatus (cosmea) – half-hardy annual
Lathyrus odoratus (sweet pea) – hardy annual
Verbena × hybrida (vervain) – half-hardy annual

The trug and secateurs are the essential tools of the flower arranger. Here a classic mixture of red tulips, yellow daffodils and assorted primula has been cut for indoor vases.

Half-hardy annual with masses of small, orchid-like flowers in a wide colour range and marked or spotted with contrasting colours.

Herbaceous perennials for cut-flowers

These versatile and diverse plants produce magnificent flowers. Herbaceous perennials to consider for cut-flowers include:

Achillea filipendula (fern-leaf yarrow): Lemon flowers in 10–15cm (4–6in) wide heads from mid- to late summer.

Catananche caerulea (cupid's dart): Button-like blue flower on long stems during early and mid-summer.

Coreopsis verticillata: Bright yellow, star-like flowers throughout summer.

Gypsophila paniculata (baby's breath): Massed white flowers in lax, clustered heads throughout summer.

Solidago – Garden Hybrids (golden rod): Distinctive, clustered heads of yellow, feathery flower heads from mid-summer to autumn.

Coloured foliage for floral arrangements

Many shrubs, climbers and herbaceous plants have variegated or single-coloured leaves that are ideal for creating extra colour in flower arrangements. For example, variegated ivies create wispy features at the fronts of arrangements, while coloured leaves of hostas provide a denser effect.

Getting the best from cut-flowers

● Do not repeatedly cut flowers from the same plant, as the garden display will be spoiled. Rather, grow a few plants in an out-of-the-way corner, and cut principally from them.
● When cutting foliage from shrubs, take it from the back of the plant.
● Do not cut flowers from plants that are wilting – their stems should be full of moisture. Usually, early in the morning is the best time to cut them.
● Cut stems at a 45-degree angle, remove lower leaves and place them in a bucket of deep, clean water in a cool, shaded room for twenty-four hours before arranging.

Culinary herb borders

Herbs are some of the oldest cultivated plants, and include annuals, biennials, herbaceous perennials and evergreen shrubs. Some herbs are grown for their leaves, which are used to flavour a wide range of dishes, while others have seeds that introduce rich, spicy flavours to food and drinks. Occasionally, roots and stems are used to create flavourings and sauces. Herbs are also used to garnish food.

Above: This classic brick-edged kitchen garden herb border exhibits a mixture of chives and feverfew with alchemilla added in.

Preparing herb borders

Herbs like well-drained but moisture-retentive soil, which is neither too acid nor alkaline, and a sunny, wind-sheltered position in the garden. Leafy herbs grow best in fertile soil, whereas herbs cultivated for their seeds do well in poor soil.

How to grow relatively low-level herbs in cartwheel formations is featured on pages 116 and 117. Here, herb growing is reserved for small beds and corner borders, perhaps near kitchen doors or adjacent to a patio.

Dig the soil about 30cm (12in) deep in autumn, remove all perennial weeds and add well-decomposed garden compost or manure. Allow the soil to settle and either sow seeds in spring or set young plants in place at the same time of year.

Herbs to grow for their leaves

Allium schoenoprasum (chives): Hardy perennial, with onion-flavoured, grass-like and tubular, green leaves that are ideal for adding to salads and to flavour foods. Plants grow 15–25cm (6–10in) high; space them 23–30cm (9–12in) apart.

Borago officinalis (borage): Hardy annual with somewhat oval, green leaves covered with silvery hairs; add young leaves to salads and fruit cups, where they introduce a cucumber-like flavour. Plants grow 45–90cm (1½–3ft) high; space them 23–30cm (9–12in) apart.

Melissa officinalis (balm): Herbaceous perennial with pale green, hairy, heart-shaped and nettle-like leaves that when bruised reveal a refreshing lemon-like bouquet. Plants grow 60cm–1.2m (2–4ft) high; space them 38–45cm (15–18in) apart.

Mentha spicata (spearmint): Spreading, herbaceous perennial with upright stems bearing leaves that reveal a spearmint-like aroma and widely used to flavour foods and drinks. Plants grow 30–60cm (1–2ft) high; they are wide-spreading and invasive.

Ruta graveolens (rue): Evergreen shrub with deeply-divided blue-green leaves; young leaves are chopped finely and added to salads. Plants grow about 60–75cm (2–2½ft) high and spread to 45cm (1½ft).

Salvia officinalis (sage): Shrubby, with wrinkled, aromatic, grey-green and slightly bitter-tasting leaves that introduce added flavour to many foods. Plants grow 45–60cm (1½–2ft) high, with a similar spread.

Thymus vulgaris (thyme): Creeping, evergreen shrub with aromatic dark green leaves employed in stuffings, in soups and with fish, casseroles and other cooked foods. Plants grow 10–20cm (4–8in) high; space young plants 23–30cm (9–12in) apart.

Herbs to grow for their seeds

Anethum graveolens (dill): Hardy annual with feathery, thread-like, anise-flavoured leaves. Seeds, with their strong anise flavour, are added to vinegar. Plants grow 60–90cm (2–3ft) high; thin seedlings to 23–30cm (9–12in) apart.

Carum carvi (caraway): Biennial with umbrella-like heads of small, green flowers. The seeds are used to flavour buns, cakes and bread. Plants grow 75cm (2½ft) high; space them 30cm (12in) apart.

Coriandrum sativum (coriander): Hardy annual with fern-like leaves and pink-mauve flowers. Seeds are added to curries and stews; the leaves are used to flavour soups and meat dishes. Plants grow 23–75cm (9–30in) high; thin seedlings to 15cm (6in) apart.

Foeniculum vulgare (fennel): Perennial with anise-flavoured seeds and thread-like, blue-green leaves. Plants grow 1.5–2.4m (5–8ft) high; space them 30–45cm (12–18in) apart.

Pimpinella anisum (aniseed): Hardy annual with large, umbrella-like flower heads bearing small, white flowers. Seeds are used to flavour food and drinks. Plants grow 45cm (1½ft) high; space them 30cm apart.

Other herbs grown for their leaves

Chervil

Hyssop

Sweet Basil

Sweet Marjoram

Tarragon

A herb to grow for its stems

Angelica archangelica (angelica): Biennial, growing 1.8–2.4m (6–8ft) high and 90cm (3ft) wide, with hollow stems and leaf stalks that can be candied. If seeds and flower heads are not wanted, cut them off when young to encourage plants to continue for another year.

A herb to grow for its roots

Armoracia rusticana (horseradish): A perennial plant grown for its roots, which when cleaned and prepared produce the well-known and pungent sauce that has been eaten with beef for centuries. Plants grow about 60cm (2ft) high and are planted 45cm (1½ft) apart.

Foliage corners

A corner packed with plants that reveal attractive leaves is a delight during summer – and often throughout the year, if evergreens are chosen. If the area is badly drained, construct a raised bed about 30cm (12in) high. Also, if the subsoil is chalky, this is an excellent way to grow shallow-rooting plants that dislike alkaline conditions.

Opposite: This spiky-leaved phormium surrounded by rampaging hostas would create a striking feature in any border.

The range of plants suitable for creating striking foliage corners is remarkably wide. Many of these plants have magnificent architectural form as well as strong colours and textures in their leaves and stems, and they are readily available in garden centres, growing in containers and ready for planting in the garden. Attractive, variously shaped and coloured foliage will always contrast well with floriferous plants and other garden features. Here are some ideas for a few herbaceous plants, annuals, biennials and grasses that go well together and that you could consider for a foliage corner in your garden.

Herbaceous plants

These are plants that reveal colourful foliage throughout summer – and sometimes into winter. There is a wide and readily available range of plants to choose from:

Alchemilla mollis **(lady's mantle):** Light green, hairy leaves surmounted from early to mid-summer by yellow-green flowers. This plant is ideal for the edge of a border.
Height: 30–45cm (1–1½ft)
Plant: 30–38cm (12–15in) apart

Heuchera **'Pewter Moon':** Leaves subtly marbled pewter above, with a deep maroon tone below.
Height: 25–38cm (10–15in)
Plant: 38–45cm (15–18in) apart

Melissa officinalis **'Aurea' (golden balm):** Golden-green, nettle-like and toothed-edged leaves.
Height: 45–60cm (1½–2ft)
Plant: 30–45cm (1–1½ft) apart

Rodgersia podophylla: Mid-green, horse-chestnut-like leaves and delicate, pale buff flowers during early and mid-summer.
Height: 90cm–1.2m (3–4ft)
Plant: 60cm (2ft) apart

Scrophularia auriculata **'Variegata'** (previously known as *S. aquatica* **'Variegata',** and popularly as variegated water figwort): Green leaves attractively splashed and covered with rich, creamy stripes.
Height: 60–90cm (2–3ft)
Plant: 38–45cm (15–18in) apart

Stachys byzantina **(lamb's tongue):** Oval, mid-green leaves densely covered with white-silver hairs that have a woolly nature.
Height: 30–45cm (1–1½ft)
Plant: 30–45cm (1–1½ft) apart

Hostas for colour

Widely known as plantain lilies, these leafy plants are ideal for smothering the ground with attractive foliage, as well as for planting in containers. Varieties for planting in large pots and tubs are described on page 60; they can also be planted in borders. However, at ground level hostas are likely to be attacked by slugs and snails.

Half-hardy annuals

Several half-hardy annuals have attractively coloured or variegated leaves. These plants are raised from seeds sown in gentle warmth in early spring and planted into borders when all risk of frost has passed. Several of them are fully described on page 25; these include *Amaranthus tricolor* (Joseph's coat), *Brassica* 'Northern Lights' (ornamental cabbage), *Bassia scoparia* 'Trichophylla' (previously known as *Kochia scoparia* 'Trichophylla', and popularly as summer cypress), *Perilla frutescens* 'Nankinensis', and *Zea mays* (ornamental sweet corn).

Ornamental grasses

These have an informal nature and are ideal for planting along the edges of raised borders, where their leaves can cascade unhindered.

Acorus gramineus 'Ogon': Perennial with long, arching leaves with golden variegated bands. It is ideal for creating colour during winter.

Hakonechloa macra 'Alboaurea': Graceful perennial with narrow leaves vividly variegated gold and buff, with touches of bronze.

Phalaris arundinacea 'Picta' (gardener's garters): Leaf blades variegated with cream and bright green stripes.

Sculptural plants

These are plants that by dint of their size, shape and texture have a dramatic influence on gardens. Some of them have giant, majestic foliage, others sword-like leaves and spartan stems, and a few have pretty, clustered flower heads.

Bold, spiky, long-leaved, dramatic or plain eccentric-looking, architectural or sculptural plants are the unsung stars of the horticultural firmament. Used imaginatively and well, they serve as the cornerstones of the garden landscape. Even a single plant can transform a dull border quickly and dramatically, keeping the garden alive and interesting at times when there may be little else to grab the attention.

Impressive foliage

The list of plants that can spur a garden with their dramatic foliage is endless, but here is a selection of the best of them:
***Acanthus spinosus* (bear's breeches):** Statuesque herbaceous perennial with large, handsome, deeply-cut and spiny, dark green leaves. Bold spikes of white and purple flowers are borne on 45cm (1½ft)

long stems during mid- and late summer.
Height: 90cm–1.2m (3–4ft)
Spread: 90cm (3ft)
Gunnera manicata **(giant rhubarb):** Slightly tender herbaceous perennial with enormous, kidney-shaped, lobed and toothed, dark green leaves, sometimes 2.4m (8ft) or more across. Only plant it in a large garden, preferably beside an informal or wildlife pond.
Height: 1.8–3m (6–10ft)
Spread: 2.4–4.5m (8–15ft)
Hosta sieboldiana **(plantain lily):** Herbaceous perennial with large, ribbed, glossy, mid-green leaves that smother the ground with foliage.
Height: 45–60cm (1½–2ft)
Spread: 45–75cm (1½–2½ft)
Rheum palmatum **'Atrosanguineum' (ornamental rhubarb):** Herbaceous perennial with upright stems bearing large, deeply-cut, purplish-red leaves. Tall stems bear deep pink or red, bead-like flowers.
Height: 1.5–2.4m (5–8ft)
Spread: 90cm–1.2m (3–4ft)

Sword-like leaves

These create dramatic features, especially around white-painted houses with an uncomplicated appearance. They also blend with patios formed of bright paving.
Yucca filamentosa **(Adam's needle):** Dramatic evergreen shrub with stiff, usually erect, glaucous and mid-green, sword-like leaves that originate from a central stem. The variegated forms have greater eye appeal and include 'Variegata', with green leaves edged in creamy-yellow. 'Bright Edge' is another variegated form.
Height: 60–75cm (2–2½ft)
Spread: 75cm–1m (2½–3ft)
Yucca gloriosa **(Spanish dagger):** Forms a dense rosette of dark green leaves at the top of a slow-growing, woody trunk. During late summer and well into autumn it bears bell-shaped, creamy-white flowers on long stalks.
Height: 90cm–1.8m (3–6ft)
Spread: 90cm–1.5m (3–5ft)

Dramatic flower heads

Flower heads bring even greater drama to sculptural plants, and some of them even look good when their flowers fade.
Euphorbia characias subsp. wulfenii: A dramatic evergreen, soft-stemmed shrub with a woody base and narrowly lance-shaped, blue-green leaves. From late spring to mid-summer it bears large, terminal clusters of bright yellow-green bracts. It looks impressive when planted at the top of a flight of steps, alongside an old, weathered wall or by a wrought-iron gate or railings.
Height: 1.2m (4ft)
Spread: 1.2m (4ft)
Lysichiton americanus **(skunk cabbage):** Moisture-loving, clump-forming herbaceous perennial with large, green leaves and flowers formed of deep golden-yellow spathes, 23–45cm (9–18in) high, during late spring and early summer. *L. camtschatcensis* has pure-white spathes. Both plants are ideal for planting in a bog garden.
Height: 60cm–1.2m (2–4ft)
Spread: 60cm (2ft)

Phormiums for gardens and tubs

Widely known as New Zealand flax, phormiums are half-hardy evergreen perennials with leathery, strap-shaped leaves; some have a single colour, while others are variegated. It is the variegated forms that are mainly grown, as they are less vigorous than the species and most grow 60–90cm (2–3ft) high and wide. Varieties to consider include:
'Cream Delight': Compact, with creamy-white leaves edged in green.
'Maori Chief': Vigorous, to 1.2m (4ft), with green, pink, red and buff leaves.
'Maori Maiden': Upright nature, with leaves 75–90cm (2½–3ft) long, reddish-pink and edged in bronze.
'Maori Queen': Erect habit, up to 1m (3ft), with pink leaves edge in purple.
'Sundowner': Wide leaves that reveal a creamy-white outer band and a greyish-purple centre.

Japanese gardens

There are few styles of garden more clinical yet as serene and calming as Japanese gardens. These gardens traditionally make extensive use of water, stone lanterns, bamboos, maples, azaleas, bridges and pagodas, but a simpler form can be created for small, enclosed gardens.

This is the so-called 'dry garden', a replica Japanese garden in which raked coarse sand or fine gravel covers the entire area and represents water, with rocks carefully positioned to create land. Additionally, distinctive plants in containers can be strategically placed to form focal points or areas of interest near paths or buildings. Shrubs and small trees can also be planted in soil at the edges, with sand raked around them. Specimens of bonsai, the ancient Japanese art of miniature plant-growing, can be displayed on low tables. Bonsai shrubs and trees are grown in small, shallow containers and kept 'dwarf' through regular pruning of their leaves, stems and roots.

Construction and maintenance

Small 'dry' gardens are easy to plan and quick to build, but sometimes they suffer from problems with weeds. When preparing the area allocated for your dry garden, remove all perennial weeds, such as docks, dandelions, couch grass and ground elder. Rake and firm the surface, then place a porous fabric or plastic sheet over the entire area. Next, place a thin layer of fine gravel or coarse sand over the top.

The surface of your Japanese garden needs to be raked regularly to create patterns in the gravel or sand and to remove debris, such as fallen leaves. Use a metal garden rake to create patterns. In ancient Japanese gardening, alternating rows of straight and wavy lines represent the flowing of a stream, while circles raked around rocks accentuate the fact that they look like islands.

Plants for dry garden containers

Acer palmatum **'Dissectum Atropurpureum'**: Forms a low, dome-headed deciduous tree with finely-cut, bronze-red leaves. *A. p.* 'Dissectum' is similar, with light green leaves. Both these small trees are ideal for planting in large tubs, or even in the ground with gravel drawn around them.
Height: 60–75cm (2–2½ft)
Spread: 1.2m (4ft)
Fargesia nitida (previously known as *Arundinaria nitida*): Hardy bamboo with purple stems that reveal a waxy bloom and bear bright green leaves. It is ideal for planting in a large, wooden planter.
Height: 1.8–2.4m (6–8ft)
Spread: Forms a clump

Coloured streams

These add a fascinating quality to Japanese gardens throughout the year and help to join one part of a garden with another. They are formed of coloured, shale-like stones that create a 'river', 90cm–1.2m (3–4ft) wide, which meanders through a garden, rather than running in a straight line. A path formed of large stepping stones passing through it gives the impression of a ford and helps to draw the eye to special features, such as bonsai specimens.

Fargesia murieliae (previously known as *Arundinaria murieliae*): Hardy bamboo with arching canes bearing dark green, narrowly lance-shaped leaves. It is ideal for planting in a large, square, wooden planter.
Height: 1.8–2.1m (6–7ft)
Spread: Forms a clump

Picea glauca **'Alberta Blue'**: Evergreen conifer, forming a dense pyramid of silvery-blue foliage.
Height: 45–60cm (1½–2ft)
Spread: 30–45cm (1–1½ft)

Pinus mugo **'Ophir'**: Evergreen conifer with a compact, rounded nature formed of dark green, gold-tipped needles that turn bright gold during winter.
Height: 60cm (2ft)
Spread: 75–90cm (2½–3ft)

Pinus strobus **'Radiata'** (previously known as *P. s.* **'Nana'**): Distinctive, slow-growing, evergreen conifer with a dignified appearance formed by dark, blue-green needles.
Height: 75–90cm (2½–3ft)
Spread: 1.2–1.5m (4–5ft)

Sasa veitchii: Hardy bamboo with large, green leaves with papery, white edges. It is ideal for planting in a large, wooden planter.
Height: 1.2–1.5m (4–5ft)
Spread: Clump-forming

Tea gardens

A tea garden was traditionally important in the ritual of Japanese tea ceremonies – an area where people would assemble and cast off worldly cares before drinking tea. The garden's purpose was to encourage serenity and to focus thoughts. The garden was uncomplicated by ephemeral flowers; instead, trees, shrubs and ferns created a timeless and serendipitous landscape. The dry garden described opposite emulates this area of the Japanese garden.

A classic Japanese garden, characterized by an ornamental pine tree, stone-paved areas and expanses of gravel.

Winter gardens

Winter-flowering plants are invaluable for brightening the so-called dull season of the year. Winter-brightening shrubs and trees with colourful barks and stems look superb on their own, but when other plants are positioned around them, their season is extended and the display improved. Here are a few combinations of plants that will bring added cheer to your garden.

Associations for early winter

With the richly-coloured leaves of autumn a blurred memory, colour in a winter garden is always welcome. For an unusual combination of white and purple – which is especially attractive in the low and fading light of a winter afternoon – plant the deciduous tree *Salix daphnoides* (violet willow) near a group of silver birches. Prune young shoots of the willow hard back in early spring to encourage the growth of colourful stems for the following winter.

Try a combination of *Hamamelis mollis* 'Pallida' (Chinese witch hazel), with pale yellow flowers faintly flushed claret-red at their centres, with a grouping of *Erica carnea* 'King George' planted in front. The rose-pink flowers of the erica associate well with the outstandingly beautiful flowers of the hamamelis, which are borne on leafless branches.

Train *Jasminum nudiflorum* (winter-flowering jasmine) against a north-facing wall and plant *Erica carnea* 'King George' in front.

Associations for mid-winter

Once Christmas has passed and the days begin to lengthen once more, the garden becomes a place of increasing cheer.

Plant the evergreen *Helleborus niger* (Christmas rose), bearing saucer-shaped white flowers, with white- or pink-flowered winter-flowering ericas (*Erica carnea*) in front of it. Use varieties such as 'Springwood Pink' (rich pink), 'Springwood White' (white) or 'Winter Beauty' (rich pink).

Grow the yellow-flowered *Jasminum nudiflorum* (winter-flowering jasmine) on a north-facing wall with a rose-pink form of the evergreen shrub *Camellia sasanqua* in front.

Plant the bulbous and purple-flowering *Crocus imperati* beneath *Hamamelis mollis* (Chinese witch hazel). It creates an attractive combination of purple and golden-yellow. This crocus naturalizes well in grass, but a large number of them are needed to create a dominant display.

Associations for late winter

With winter's worst weather fading and spring waiting to break, this is an exciting and bright time in the garden. In some

Plan a winter-flowering border

Easy access and direct viewing are most desirable when planning a winter-flowering garden. Borders are best positioned beside a patio or in a secluded but accessible corner, and if a garden seat is placed near the plants it makes them an even greater asset to the garden.

areas, however, the perfidious nature of weather slows things up, and some of these combinations of plants will appear in early spring, rather than late winter.

- The tuberous-rooted *Eranthis hyemalis* (winter aconite), with its lemon-yellow flowers, is ideal for planting under silver birches.
- Naturalize the bulbous *Crocus chrysanthus* in large drifts under silver birches.
- Plant *Primula* 'Wanda', with dark red-purple flowers, around *Rhododendron × praecox*, which reveals rose-purple flowers.
- Plant the bulbous, bright royal-blue *Iris histrioides* in front of the late winter or early spring-flowering *Forsythia suspensa*, which reveals bright yellow, pendulous flowers. The forsythia is ideal for planting against a sunny wall, which encourages earlier flowering.
- For a plant combination in a woodland garden, try a white-flowered form of the bulbous *Erythronium dens-canis* (dog's-tooth violet) with the deep-blue and bulbous *Scilla bifolia*. Plant each in dominant clumps.

The winter-flowering jasmine (*Jasminum nudiflorum*) offers a colourful background to other plants throughout much of winter, and none is more deserving than the well-known *Rhododendron* 'Christmas Cheer', which we are now instructed to call 'Ima-shojo'. It has blush-pink flowers that last longer in cool, partial shade than strong sunlight, and combine perfectly with the yellow of the jasmine.

Below: A typical winter border, featuring the highly-coloured stems of *Cornus alba* (dogwood), *Helleborus foetidus* in the foreground and a mixture of different heathers and ivies.

Quick-fix Ideas to Brighten Gardens

Making a garden more exciting and attractive is not always about creating new features, but more often than not about improving existing and established areas. For example, patios and lawns take up the most space in the majority of gardens, and should these become tatty and neglected the entire garden is marred. Broken or loose paving slabs on a patio, or bare areas in lawns, are eyesores that ruin the effect of the garden overall; gravel drives become pot-holed and waterlogged; border edges become ragged and shrubs overgrow – but all can be quickly corrected, to remarkable effect.

There are, of course, quick and easy features that can also be added to a garden to create interest instantly, and several ideas are given here.

Smartening patios, paths and drives

Tatty paths and loose, cracked patio stones are an eyesore that let the garden down badly.

Loose paving slabs: Paving slabs often become dislodged. Carefully lift off the slab and chisel away the cement that secured it. Use a mixture of one part Portland cement powder to six of building sand; form five blobs, each about 7.5cm (3in) wide, in the corners and centre. Replace the slab and gently but firmly tap with a large piece of wood. Fill the cracks with a slightly moist mixture of one part Portland cement and three parts building sand.

Broken or sunken 'flexible' paving bricks: These bricks are laid on a bed of sharp sand; sometimes, individual bricks become broken, or small areas depressed.

Use the point of a trowel to prise up the damaged brick (or bricks). Add more sharp sand to the area and replace the bricks. Use a plank of wood and a club hammer to tap the bricks level with the surrounding surface. Brush sharp sand between the bricks.

Cracks in concrete: Eventually, concrete patios and paths crack, especially if the foundations are weak and the area is prone to subsidence. Chip off damaged cement from the crack, so that a clean fracture is created. Use a moist mixture of one part Portland cement and three of building sand; pack this into the crack and use a trowel to smooth the surface.

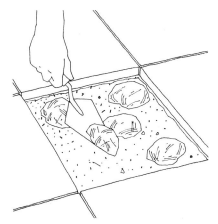

Loose paving slabs are easily repaired; lift out the slab and remove the concrete from the slab and base (see opposite).

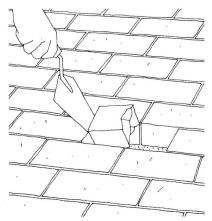

Broken 'pavers' in patios, drives and paths formed of flexible paving can be quickly replaced (see opposite).

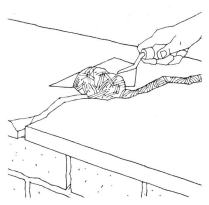

Cracks in concrete steps and along the edges of patios are unsightly and dangerous. To repair, see below.

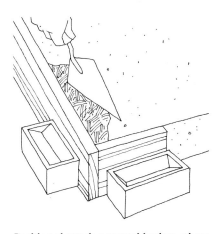

Position shuttering around broken edges to paths and steps. Remove broken concrete and make a repair (see below).

Wet depressions often occur in gravel drives in winter. A repair is quickly made by digging out the wet area (see below).

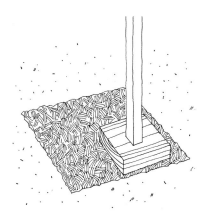

Oil dripping from cars soon damages macadam drives. To make a repair, follow the instructions below.

Damaged edges to concrete paths and steps: The edges of concrete paths and steps often chip, becoming unsightly and dangerous. Clear away loose concrete and brush the edges with a weak PVA adhesive. When this glue is tacky, position a piece of wood alongside the edge. Pack a mixture of one part Portland cement and five of ballast, plus a little PVA, into the broken area. Leave the wood in position for at least three weeks, until the repair is firmly set.

Depressions and puddles in gravel drives: Rake clean gravel away from the area, then remove the mixture of mud and gravel. Fork over the base and mix in a dusting of Portland cement. Firm this and return the gravel.

Depressions in macadam drives: If the damaged area is small, use a club hammer and wide metal chisel to cut around the area; remove the asphalt to about 5cm (2in) deep. Paint the base and edges with bitumen. When this has dried, add a thin layer of cold asphalt and compress it with a heavy piece of wood. Continue to add asphalt in layers, firming each one until the surface is level.

Making a cartwheel herb garden

Herbs can be grown in many places in the garden – as part of a vegetable plot, in beds near the kitchen door or in containers. But for a real herb feature, why not construct a simple cartwheel herb garden?

Opposite: This neatly planted herb cartwheel incorporates a sundial for added effect. The blue-painted wooden dial of the device looks smart and contrasts effectively with the surrounding gravel.

Step-by-step to creating a cartwheel herb garden

During winter, dig an area 1.8–2.4m (6–8ft) square; mix in well-decomposed compost.
- In spring, rake the area level. Systematically tread over the surface.
- To mark a circle, use a piece of string 60–75cm (2–2½ft) long tied to a cane at each end. Insert one cane in the centre of the proposed cartwheel area, then scribe a line to indicate the rim.
- Mark the positions of the spokes, as well as the hub – form a circle 23–30cm (9–12in) wide at the centre.
- If the planting areas are too large, use pebbles to divide them into inner and outer segments.
- Water the plants, while still in their pots, the day before planting them.
- Position the plants (still in their pots) and adjust them into an attractive display.
- Use a trowel to plant the herbs.
- Water the plants to settle them in.

Plants for cartwheel herb gardens

Low-growing herbs with attractive leaves create the best displays; tall types, such as sage, can be kept low by pinching off the tips of shoots to encourage bushiness.

Constraining some herbs to the confines of a cartwheel is against their nature, so be prepared to replant the wheel after three years with young plants. Here are a few herbs to consider:

Chives: Perennial, with grass-like, tubular, green leaves and rose-pink flowers during early and mid-summer.
Mints: Range of perennial plants with attractive leaves. They are invasive.
Parsley: A biennial usually grown as a hardy annual, with bright green foliage.
Rosemary: Evergreen shrub, with aromatic, dark green leaves and mauve flowers mainly in spring.
Sage: Shrubby with grey-green leaves; it is the variegated forms that create the most spectacular displays.
Thyme: Creeping, evergreen, mat-forming shrub with dark green leaves. Several forms, with coloured leaves: *Thymus × citriodorus* 'Aureus' (golden leaves); *T. × C.* 'Silver Queen' (variegated leaves).

Chessboard variation

This is an ideal way to grow herbs, especially those with a low and mat-forming nature. Position 45cm (1½ft) square alternately-coloured paving slabs to form a chess board design. Plant herbs in the gaps between the slabs. An attractive design can be created with coloured-leaved herbs.

The quick way to construct a cartwheel herb garden

The full account is given opposite, but these diagrams summarize the key steps:

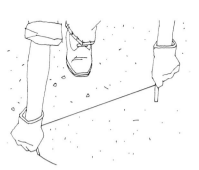

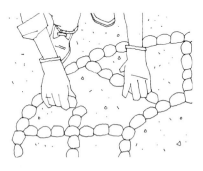

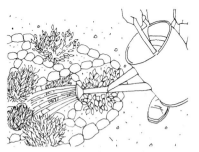

1 Mark out the area allocated for the herb cartwheel, using twine and bamboo canes. Plan the individual herb segments as evenly as possible.

2 Press pebbles firmly into the soil to delineate individual herb segments, dividing up into smaller ones for a larger range of small herbs.

3 Position the plants and, when you are satisfied with them, use a trowel to plant them. Water the plants and cover the surface with gravel.

Special edgings

Installing a new edging instantly tidies up the periphery of a border and makes you feel good about your garden. Some edging designs have a rigid, formal appearance, while others are more relaxed and informal.

Above: This mixed border has been edged with a double row of large, smooth pebbles. The stones complement the natural stone path beautifully and give the border a real lift.

Wooden edgings

Wooden border and lawn edgings have a lovely, natural appearance and are especially useful for brightening informal areas. They can be quickly and easily constructed from either ordinary logs or longer and more elegant log rolls.

Log edgings: These are ideal for edging gravel paths, grass paths and informal borders in woodland gardens. They are easily installed; use a spade to form a uniform depression one-third the thickness of the log. Preferably, use logs about 1.5m (5ft) long; if less than this, and when relatively thin, they are easily dislodged.

In woodland gardens, these edgings are ideal for combining with log steps (see page 53).

Log rolls: These can be used to create edgings alongside borders and where the soil is slightly higher than the level of the path. They are ideal for edging paths which have a serpentine nature.

Log rolls are formed of 1m (3ft) long rolls of logs, 7.5–10cm (3–4in) thick and cut lengthways. They are usually secured

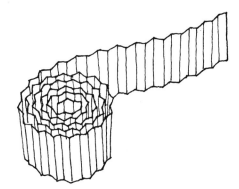

A corrugated plastic-roll edging is cheap, malleable, versatile and attractive.

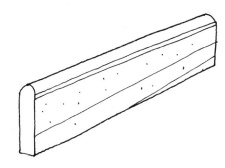

Straight stone edges will grace any garden border – as long as it is straight...

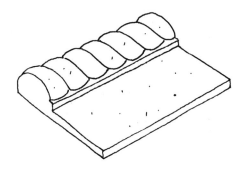

A sculptured or fluted stone edging is reminiscent of Victorian gardens.

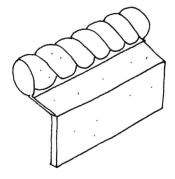

This 'coiled rope' stone edging has a mowing strip built into it, for easier mowing.

A path with a log edging looks smart if informal, evoking woodland parks and nature reserves. The path itself should be coated with bark chippings to reinforce the natural effect.

together by two pieces of strong but pliable wire and are available in several different heights, including 15cm (6in), 23cm (9in) and 30cm (12in).

To install log rolls as edgings, use a spade to cut a narrow trench to a depth of about one-third of the roll's height. Unfurl the log roll and slot it in place; then, firm soil around its base.

Timber edgings: These are constructed of timbers of varying thicknesses; those to form an edging between a gravel drive and a flowerbed would need to be about 10cm (4in) wide and 5cm (2in) thick. Additionally, they would need to be thoroughly treated with a preservative.

Unlike log-rolls, these edgings are not suitable for borders with meandering edges. Timber edgings are relatively quick to install, as they do not need to be cemented into

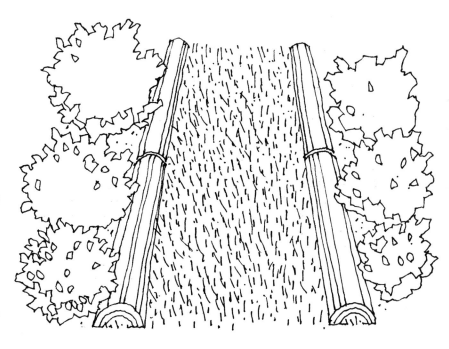

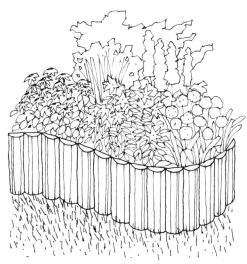

Above: This smart herringbone brick path immediately lifts the lawn it encircles.

Above right: It is possible to create a raised bed by using upright sawn logs or old railway sleepers embedded in the ground. They make a striking effect.

position. Instead, secure them with stout wooden pegs banged into the soil.

Plastic edgings

Plastic edgings are not always the most elegant of garden embellishments, although increasingly they can be found in a variety of different styles and colours. The most popular type of plastic edging is corrugated for maximum strength and comes in green. It is available in several depths (usually 15–20cm (6–8in) and in

rolls holding a strip about 7.5m (25ft) long. It is installed by using a spade to form a slit alongside a border, then inserting the strip to about one-third of its depth. However, because the edging is corrugated it is difficult to produce a formal, straight edge. It is therefore best reserved for informal areas.

Concrete edgings

For a long-life edging, concrete has few rivals, especially alongside gravel drives where there is always the risk of car wheels trespassing on a border. Concrete edging strips, 90cm (3ft) long, 15cm (6in) deep and about 5cm (2in) thick, are readily available and can be quickly cemented into position. Position this edging so that its top is 25–36mm (1–1¼in) above the gravel's surface, with the rest cemented into the ground.

Edging tiles

These are increasingly popular as they offer the chance to create a personalized and distinctive garden.

Edging tiles take longer to install than most edgings, and for long-term stability they need a concrete base and cementing into position. Nevertheless, an afternoon's work is rewarded by a neat edging.

Smartening up garden furniture

Spring is a time of rejuvenation, when plants of all kinds send up fresh shoots. It is also the time to get out garden furniture and smarten it up...

Plastic furniture becomes dull after a winter in a shed: use a proprietary plastic cleaner.

Use a quick-drying spray paint to smarten cane furniture; choose a windless day and place the furniture on newspapers.

Rub down wood and re-varnish; this needs a dry day to prevent the varnish clouding.

Finally, use either a patio-cleaning chemical to remove moss from patios, or a high-pressure hose (but take care not to direct it onto colour-washed walls).

Smartening lawns

A handsome lawn acts as an attractive foil for flowering and foliage plants and is usually the first feature to be noticed on entering a garden. However, it is often the most abused of all garden features, having to survive the full force of the weather and the ravages of dogs and children.

Fortunately, there are many quick and easy ways to repair what should be the emerald glory at the heart of your garden. How to repair broken edgings, holes, bumps and hollows is described on page 18; here are a few quick-fix ideas for more easily-solved problems.

Ravages of dogs: Dogs have a propensity for digging holes in lawns and ripping away the surface grass, while bitches tend to urinate all over lawns, causing yellow patches wherever they go. Small holes can be treated by replacing the damaged area with a piece of fresh turf, but urine-stained, yellow areas require different treatment, although of course they too can simply be replaced with a piece of fresh grass. However, usually, it is more practical to dig out an infected area, replace it with fresh soil and then sow fresh grass seed (this is best done in spring or late summer). If the area to be treated is only a little yellow, use a garden fork to spike the ground, then repeatedly and thoroughly water the lawn. Later, apply a lawn fertilizer to the area to encourage the growth of fresh grass.

Worn, bare patches: These are often the result of too much foot traffic – or even a path in a wrong place so that people take the shortest route instead of walking by a circuitous way.

Sometimes, grass can be encouraged to grow more quickly and abundantly by fencing off the bare area or placing wire-netting over it. Keeping the area moist assists grass to grow.

If the soil is seriously compacted, fork it to about 15cm (6in) deep; re-firm it and sprinkle seed across the area at 50g sq. m. (1½oz sq. yd). Lightly rake the seed into the surface, then gently but thoroughly water the area. Allow the soil to dry slightly, then cover with clear polythene; remove it when the grass is 18–25mm (¾–1in) high. Keep the area fenced off until the grass is well established.

Contending with tree roots: Sometimes, the roots of trees push above the lawn's surface and interfere with grass cutting. In an informal lawn, use a strimmer to cut grass over the roots. Alternatively, in formal lawns, one solution is to form a round, raised bed flowerbed or paved area around the tree.

Dealing with weeds: Weeds will quickly take command of lawns that have been poorly prepared, created from weed-infested turf, or neglected for many years. Regular mowing, thorough watering, yearly feeding and careful scarifying will, eventually, eradicate most weeds. Weed-killing chemicals can be applied but must be used with care and consideration.

The quick way to remove lawn dew

In late summer and autumn, overnight dew sometimes sits on the grass for hours in the morning, preventing mowing until it has dried. Use a long garden cane with a whippy end to swish over the lawn's surface and knock off the dew, encouraging the lawn to dry out quickly.

Time & money-saving tips

Saving time and money with plants in containers and herbaceous borders, as well as with roses.

Plants in containers

Removing dead flowers: Summer-flowering plants in hanging-baskets, windowboxes, troughs and other containers can be brightened up quickly by using sharp scissors to snip off dead flowers. This extends their flowering period and prevents decaying flowers spreading infection to others.

Where daily watering is difficult: Add water-retaining materials to the compost when planting the container. Use moisture-retaining liners when planting a hanging-basket.

Easy watering: When watering hanging-baskets, or a large group of pots, tie the end of a hosepipe to a 1.2m (4ft) long cane. It is then possible to direct the water more easily into pots: when watering a hanging-basket, bend over the tip of the hosepipe (it can be held in place with a piece of wire, perhaps from a wire clothes hanger). Alternatively, use proprietary hosepipe fittings.

Recycling growing-bags: Where a growing-bag has been used to grow vegetables, perhaps tomatoes in a greenhouse or lettuces on a patio, at the end of the season remove the plants and place the bag in a shed. In the following spring, mix a general fertilizer with the compost and plant with culinary herbs, such as mints that need to have their roots constricted. Half-hardy annuals can also be planted in this medium.

Rejuvenating dry hanging-baskets: Where the compost in a hanging-basket has become exceptionally dry, lower the basket and immerse the compost in a large bowl or bucket of water. Wait until air bubbles

cease to rise, then replace the basket on its supporting bracket.

First-aid watering: During very hot days – or when a hanging-basket cannot be watered – place a few ice cubes on the compost. These will melt gradually and the water will become available to the plants.

Grouping plants in pots: Position plants in pots in a group, rather than spreading them over a large area. This helps to create a more impressive display, as well as slightly reducing the amount and frequency of water they require.

Keeping herbaceous borders smart and tidy

Removing dead flowers: Cutting off dead flowers is time-consuming, but it certainly prolongs the display as well as preventing plants developing seeds at the expense of growth and flowers. Use sharp secateurs or scissors and cut them immediately above a leaf. Place the dead flowers on a compost heap rather than just dropping them on the soil.

Supporting plants: Some herbaceous plants are self-supporting (see page 20), while others need unobtrusive support. The traditional way to support herbaceous plants is to push twiggy sticks around them while they are still small, so that foliage and flowers grow through them. Proprietary metal supports are available.

Mulching the soil: In spring, shallowly fork around established plants, removing weeds and ensuring that the soil does not have a crusty cap that prevents air and water entering the ground. Thoroughly water the soil, then form a 5cm (2in) thick mulch of well-decayed garden compost over the

If you are interested in saving money and basic conservation, then put old industrial containers to good use by painting them and planting them up with your favourite garden brighteners.

surface. Alternatively, use a mulch formed of shredded bark.

Autumn tidiness: During autumn, herbaceous plants die down to soil-level; the old stems can be cut down to soil-level, removed and added to a compost heap. This creates a smart and tidy border throughout winter.

Alternatively, the stems and old leaves are left in place throughout winter, so that they create an attractive feature when covered in frost.

Re-firm plants in spring: In spring, use the heel of your boot to firm soil around herbaceous plants planted during the previous autumn. This ensures soil is in close contact with the roots and that growth will begin as soon as the weather allows.

Checking out roses

Firming roses in spring: In early spring, re-firm soil around rose bushes planted during the previous year. This is especially necessary in windswept and generally exposed areas.

Dead-heading roses: Cut stems to slightly above the second or third leaf below a dead flower. Do not dead-head shrub roses grown for their hips (fruits).

Removing suckers: During summer, remove sucker shoots growing from below soil-level. Carefully scrape away soil and trace the sucker to its base. Wear a stout glove and pull off the sucker, close to its base. Replace soil and firm it around the root; loose soil encourages the development of further suckers.

Time & money-saving tips (2)

Saving time and money with hedges, shrubs and trees, and garden equipment.

Tidying up hedges

Shaping hedges: In areas where heavy snow falls are an annual occurrence, trim the tops of hedges with a slight slope so that snow has a better chance of falling off. Hedges are severely damaged when a thick covering of snow causes the branches to spread open or the whole hedge to bend over.

Bases of hedges: Always remove hedge clippings and ensure that the base does not become thick with them. If left, they reduce the circulation of air and encourage the presence of pests and diseases; they also make the hedge unsightly.

Shrubs

New shrubs for old: Shrubs with low-growing branches can be inexpensively increased by layering a few branches. During late summer or early autumn, lower a pliable, healthy shoot to soil-level and peg it into a shallow trench, 7.5–10cm (3–4in) deep and 23–45cm (9–18in) from the shoot's tip. Either cut a tongue on the shoot's lower side and about 30cm (12in) from its tip, or cut half-way around the stem and remove part of the bark. Use a stout peg to hold the shoot in place. Firm soil around the stem. Rooting takes about a year – sometimes longer.

New heathers for old: Heathers, ericas and daboecias which are old and have become bare at their centres can be encouraged to produce new plants by forming a mound of friable soil in their centres. This is best performed in autumn or spring. Work the soil between the stems and then thoroughly water the entire plant. Later,

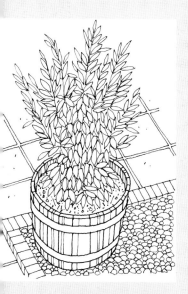

Shrubs in tubs look good anywhere in the garden – and can help keep people off cobbled areas, as in this case – but they need careful protection in the winter months.

when the stems have developed roots, dig up the complete plant and cut off the rooted parts. If small, plant them into a nursery bed until they are established.

Tender shrubs in tubs: Tender shrubs in tubs on patios may require protection from cold winter winds. In early winter, insert three canes into compost at the edge of the tub and form them into a wigwam. Tie their tops together. Then, spread a thin layer of straw around them, so that the shrub is cocooned. Tie a piece of string to the base of a cane and wind it upwards in a spiral, so that it holds the straw in place. Remove the canes and straw in late winter.

Shrubs in tubs: The compost in tubs often becomes too wet in winter. To prevent this happening and damaging a shrub's roots, cover the compost with polythene held in place by encircling the tub with string. Check that water runs towards the rim of tub, and not to the centre.

Trees

Wind damage: Fierce winds sometimes loosen 'ties' securing a trunk to a supporting stake. If the stake is undamaged, an improvised 'tie' can be made with a couple of old stockings or a pair of tights; make sure that the trunk does not rub against the stake.

Broken stakes: Where a vertical stake is broken, remove it and replace it with an H-shaped or an obliquely-angled stake. An H-shaped support is formed by two vertical stakes being knocked into the ground, 23–30cm (9–12in) either side of the trunk, and a stake then being tied between them and to the trunk.

Another way to proceed is to knock an oblique stake into the ground, about 38cm (15in) from the trunk, at an angle of 45 degrees and with its top pointing towards the prevailing wind. Tie the top part of the stake to the trunk.

Heavy fruit crops: These often weigh down branches and, occasionally, break them. Lift up the branch and use a Y-shaped prop to hold it in place.

Removing a large branch: Always cut off a large branch a few feet at a time; never immediately cut it close to the trunk.

Heavy snow falls: These soon damage branches, bending them down and causing the tree or shrub to become deformed. Consequently, always carefully remove snow either by gently tapping the branches or by using a soft brush.

Garden equipment

Lawn mowers: Regular cleaning after each use is essential for long-term, trouble-free grass cutting with a mower. First, disconnect the cable from the power supply if the mower is an electric type, or turn off the fuel supply if petrol-driven. Use a stiff brush or rag to remove grass clippings and other debris. Dry the surfaces and wipe bright-metal parts with an oily rag.

Store a petrol-driven mower in a dry shed or garage (place it on blocks of wood to prevent blades being damaged – this will also keep the machine off a damp floor). Light, hover-type mowers can be hung up.

At the end of each mowing season, thoroughly check the blades for alignment and damage. Also, check cables and plugs.

Strimmers: Nylon cord strimmers (sometimes known as 'nylon cord trimmers') are popular, efficient and ideal for cutting long grass, especially when in awkward corners, on steep banks and around trees (but do not damage the bark). They are invariably powered by mains electricity; check that a power breaker (R.C.D.) is fitted into the circuit.

After each use, wipe clean and check that there is enough nylon cord left for the next use. It can be exceptionally irritating to run out of cord halfway through a job.

Chain saws: These are lethal tools and only the experienced and confident gardener should use one. There are electric- and petrol-powered types; the former is the one most often used by home gardeners. If you use a chain saw, always observe the following do's and don'ts:

Do wear protective clothing and goggles to protect your eyes.

Do regularly check the chain's tension.

Don't use the saw above waist height.

Don't stand on a ladder, pair of steps or a box to use the saw.

Don't use the saw unless you have a companion with you holding the log being cut.

Garden safety

Gardens are one of life's joys, bringing pleasure throughout the year. But they are also full of accidents waiting to happen, if you work in a cavalier or unthinking manner and do not take the trouble to observe some basic rules.

Eyes: When using chain saws, electrical hedge-trimmers and strimmers, wear protective goggles. Also, fit safety caps to the tops of bamboo canes to prevent them damaging eyes as you bend over.

Hands: There are gloves to protect your hands, whatever the job being tackled. Where there are cats in a garden it is advisable to wear gloves when cultivating the soil or putting in plants.

Feet: Use stout, non-slip boots when using a hover-type lawn mower.

Knees: Use knee-pads to protect knees when kneeling or cutting logs. Kneelers help to protect knees, as well as making it easier for elderly people to kneel.

Electricity in the garden: Always use cables and fittings suitable for outdoor use. Additionally, use a circuit-breaker .

Garden tools: Almost every garden tool could be considered a weapon, from a garden knife to a spade. Therefore, great care should always be taken when using them. There are many unpleasant accidents waiting to befall the careless gardener, from a fork through the foot to burning a hand.

Index

Whatever you do to your garden to improve and enhance it – whichever short cuts you use – always look for inspiration in the beauty that occurs naturally as the seasons turn and plants mature.

Acknowledgements

The author and publishers would like to thank the following for their contribution to this book:

The Garden Picture Library, for all photographs except:
Jerry Harpur: p 26; p 44; p 120; p 123;
Marcus Harpur: p 38;
David Squire: p 29; p 99; p 108; p 128.

Ian Sidaway for all artwork.

Produced by Focus Publishing, The Courtyard, 26 London Road, Sevenoaks, Kent TN13 1AP (Tel: 01732 742456)